About Island Press

Since 1984, the nonprofit organization Island Press has been stimulating, shaping, and communicating ideas that are essential for solving environmental problems worldwide. With more than 1,000 titles in print and some 30 new releases each year, we are the nation's leading publisher on environmental issues. We identify innovative thinkers and emerging trends in the environmental field. We work with world-renowned experts and authors to develop cross-disciplinary solutions to environmental challenges.

Island Press designs and executes educational campaigns, in conjunction with our authors, to communicate their critical messages in print, in person, and online using the latest technologies, innovative programs, and the media. Our goal is to reach targeted audiences—scientists, policy makers, environmental advocates, urban planners, the media, and concerned citizens—with information that can be used to create the framework for long-term ecological health and human well-being.

Island Press gratefully acknowledges major support from The Bobolink Foundation, Caldera Foundation, The Curtis and Edith Munson Foundation, The Forrest C. and Frances H. Lattner Foundation, The JPB Foundation, The Kresge Foundation, The Summit Charitable Foundation, Inc., and many other generous organizations and individuals.

The opinions expressed in this book are those of the author(s) and do not necessarily reflect the views of our supporters.

Leadership for Sustainability

Leadership for Sustainability

STRATEGIES FOR TACKLING WICKED PROBLEMS

R. Bruce Hull

David P. Robertson and Michael Mortimer

 **ISLAND**PRESS | Washington | Covelo

Library of Congress Control Number: 2020941234

All Island Press books are printed on environmentally responsible materials.

Manufactured in the United States of America
10 9 8 7 6 5 4 3 2

Keywords: Anthropocene, career development, climate change, collaboration, direction-alignment-commitment theory of leadership, environmental security, leadership skills, leadership training, risk management, sustainable development, wicked problems

About the cover image: Utah's Green River flows south across the Tavaputs Plateau (top) before entering Desolation Canyon (center). The Canyon slices through the Roan and Book Cliffs—two long, staircase-like escarpments. Nearly as deep as the Grand Canyon, Desolation Canyon is one of the largest unprotected wilderness areas in the American West.

Contents

Preface

We wrote this book for people working on the consequential challenges of sustainable development and environmental security. These challenges go by various names: climate change, poverty and social unrest, food and water security, corporate responsibility, virus pandemics, rapid urbanization, threatened biodiversity, and supply chain vulnerability. Organizations in all sectors—business, government, military, nongovernmental, nonprofit, faith-based, and community—are scrambling to respond. You likely work for (or aspire to work for) one of these organizations, or you may want to better understand your roles and impacts as a consumer and a community member. We've learned from working with people like you that the skills and practices discussed in this book can help society make progress on these challenges, turning many of them into opportunities, and we've seen how these skills and practices increase the influence and career success of professionals.

A few words about the book's evolution and authorship: we (Bruce, David, and Michael) have collaborated for over a decade on this topic, building education programs and professional development opportunities focused on equipping environmental and sustainability professionals with the credentials, competencies, connections, and confidence they need to be effective. In 2010, we adopted the phrase "leadership for sustainability" as the direction and guiding theme for an executive graduate education program that has been the primary test bed and incubator for the ideas and practices described in this book. In 2014, we founded the Center for Leadership in Global Sustainability with the mission to educate, inspire, and empower professionals. Our graduate education programs and the Center created opportunities for us to work with professionals, students, and organizations from all walks of life and from around the world on challenges and opportunities of sustainable development.

Bruce is the primary author of the book, generating the initial content, writing the multiple drafts, doing the primary research on the case studies, and ensuring that the book has a consistent tone and voice. David and Michael contributed by shaping and testing ideas, as well as editing and framing the arguments. For many paragraphs, it is hard to know where one person's ideas and words end and another's begin.

We are grateful for the many people who helped shape the ideas presented in this book. First, let us recognize Jerry Abrams, who has brought both clarity and rigor to our thinking about leadership. Also let us recognize Elizabeth Hurley, who conducted primary research for the Carbon Farming case study, and substantively revised each chapter. We also owe huge debts to other colleagues with whom we collaborate on teaching this material: Holly Wise, Patty Raun, Marc Stern, Emily Talley, Paul Wagner, Courtney Kimmel, Andrew Perlstein, Rich Dooley, Joe Maroon, Jason Pearson, Janet Ranganathan, and Seth Brown. We also want to thank people who have taken the time to read drafts and suggest revisions, including Max Stephenson, Kathy Miller Perkins, Bruce Goldstein, Valerie Winrow, Angel Kwok, and Sara Alexander. A special thanks to Keith Goyden and Chicu Lokgariwar, for hosting Hull in India. The view of the Himalayas from their porch gave Hull the inspiration for the connect/collaborate/adapt framework. And, as importantly, we want to thank the students and clients in our courses and programs who continually impress us with their commitment and questions, and inspire us with their hope for the future and willingness to make a difference. It's been a privilege to be part of their learning journey and career development. And, to you, the readers of this book: we are honored to be part of your journey.

Of course, we want to acknowledge the people and organizations that opened their doors and let us document leadership in action: Arlin Wasserman of Changing Tastes; KanaPrina of JBF; Rich Dooley of Arlington County Government; Alisa Gravitz of Green America; Russ Gaskin of Co-Creative; Greg Cannito of Corvias; and Seth Brown of Storm and Stream Solutions, Brian Macnamara of Host Hotels & Resorts, as well as Bruce Goldstein, Will Butler, and Lynn Decker for help understanding the Fire Learning Network. Different versions of the case studies in Chapters 11 and 15 have been published in *Solutions*, a journal for a sustainable and desirable future.

We also owe a great debt to Island Press for taking a chance on a leadership book, and especially to our editor, Courtney Lix, whose insights and perspectives shaped and improved the book. Thanks also to Anne Kerns who designed the book's figures.

And most importantly, thank you to our families, especially our spouses and children, who support us in our work and give meaning to our lives.

We finished writing this book as COVID-19 was disrupting lives and livelihoods. The pandemic provides a sobering illustration of the book's two major lessons: (1) the Anthropocene is a time of unprecedented change, risk, and interdependency and (2) good leadership has never been more necessary. It is with great humility that we hope capacities built by this book support the collective actions needed to sustain development and security.

CHAPTER 1

Introduction

Career success and professional impact, as well as the hope and promise of sustainable development, increasingly depend on skills and practices that help solve wicked problems—skills and practices that this book calls wicked leadership. Wicked problems are extraordinarily difficult to define and even more difficult to solve. Traditional problem-solving tools, such as technology, expertise, rationality, and authority, are not up to the task. Wicked problems are wicked in large part because people are both the cause and the solution. As humanity increasingly dominates the biosphere, more and more challenges will be wicked.

Solving wicked problems requires three sets of leadership skills and practices explained and illustrated in the chapters that follow—the abilities to connect, collaborate, and adapt (Figure 1.1). Specifically, leadership skills and practices are needed to help people *connect* and coordinate the actions with others whom they may never meet, don't have authority over, and may not even know exist: people located in different organizations, sectors, time zones, countries, and supply chains. Also, skills and practices are needed to help people *collaborate* across widening differences of opinion, identity, expertise, and culture—differences being fueled by filter bubbles, echo chambers, network propaganda, confirmation bias, and motivated reasoning. And, skills and leadership practices are needed to help people *adapt* to confounding uncertainty and accelerating change, avoid analysis-paralysis, fail forward, and learn by doing.

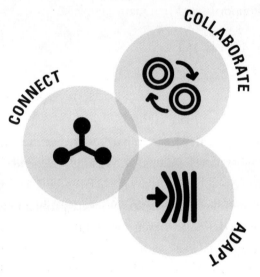

Figure 1.1. Wicked leadership. The three types of leadership practices needed for wicked situations.

Importantly, you can practice wicked leadership, regardless of your position, whether you are the person in charge at the top of your organization's hierarchy, a midlevel professional in your company's organizational chart, or a stakeholder engaging in a community planning effort where no one has authority over others. Moreover, wicked leadership skills and practices can be learned; they are not an outcome of genetics or upbringing. You can learn wicked leadership skills and practices by reading this book.

Embracing Wickedness

Environmental and sustainability professionals working in business, government, and nonprofit organizations of all scales, from local to transnational, use and need wicked leadership. To be successful and relevant, these professionals must embrace global interconnectivity, take a long-term view, navigate polarizing conflict, and manage unpredictable risks and opportunities that many people ignore, including climate, water, poverty, economic development, human rights, public health, and supply chain vulnerabilities.

If you work, or aspire to work, within an organization and community on these sorts of challenges and opportunities, then this book is intended for you. Although the book targets professionals that address environmental and sustainability challenges specifically, it provides examples, practices, and principles that will help anyone influence wicked situations they confront in their workplace and in their community. For example, later in the book we provide stories illustrating wicked leadership in the following situations:

- Imagine that you are trying to influence fickle and distracted consumers to change what they buy and what they eat in ways that reduce environmental impact and promote sustainable development. You know that facts don't convince most people to act, so you use *choice editing* and *identity management* to drive change. This story explores how chefs and foodservice professionals use these strategies to alter menus and recipes that change diets and reduce environmental impacts of conventional food and agriculture systems, especially meat production.
- Imagine that you are working with talented and motivated people from multiple organizations and communities and you come up with a great plan that, if implemented, will reduce water risks,

empower women and girls, alleviate the ravages of poverty, improve sanitation and public health, and otherwise change communities for the better. But like many good plans, it risks sitting on the shelf and gathering dust. How do you translate all that good energy and hard work into action? This story describes how a small nongovernmental organization helped rural villages in arid, poverty-stricken regions of India generate the *direction*, *alignment*, and *commitment* needed to build and restore source water management systems that dramatically improve villagers' access to water and their quality of life.

- Imagine that wildfires and other forms of human-induced climate change impacts are destroying biodiversity and human communities because the people and organizations that need to collaborate are mired in inertia, skepticism, and inaction. This story explains *trust building* and *community of practice* strategies that helped these stakeholders learn by doing and coordinate action across dozens of organizations and large regions of North America.

- Imagine that you are one of the many stakeholders in a city's effort to mitigate climate change; perhaps a real estate developer, city planner, or member of a local civic organization. The many stakeholders who need to coordinate their actions have different agendas, competing and overlapping capacities, and limited tolerance for change; and most, such as residents and commuters, aren't easily engaged. This story explains how one city is using *collective impact* strategies to make these connections and reduce its greenhouse gas emissions by 75 percent.

- Imagine that you want to improve the sustainability of your organization's operations and supply chains. You need to coordinate the actions of many widely distributed stakeholders, including investors, customers, and employees in different facilities around the world, as well as the siloed internal divisions of your company, such as engineering and finance. You don't have direct authority over any of the people you want to influence. Many of the stakeholders will never meet one another, and some won't realize they are connected to the sustainability goals you are advancing. Leadership strategies such as *accountability* and *transparency* work in this situation, and this story explains why and how a major multinational corporation and a global investment advisory service use them to lead industry-wide change.

- Imagine trying to trigger a large-scale change needed to limit global warming below 2 degrees Celsius. You convene a group of entrepreneurs to engage in *collaborative innovation*. You target soil, where most of the world's carbon is stored. This story explains a carbon farming initiative with the potential to sequester enough carbon to significantly alter the world's total greenhouse gas budget.

- Imagine that your community does not have the resources to manage the floods and pollution caused when storms overwhelm its infrastructure. This story illustrates how a community used a public–private *partnership* strategy to provide benefits, such as local jobs, as well as green infrastructure to manage its stormwater, create open space, and save money.

The Anthropocene

We live at a time when humans dominate the planet, including the climate, and are remaking life on Earth in our own image. It is a time of accelerating change, confounding uncertainty, great risk, and enormous opportunity.

Over the past few decades, real incomes in low- and middle-income countries have doubled, poverty rates have halved, two billion people have gained access to healthy drinking water, and maternal mortality has dropped by half. Today, almost as many girls get educated as boys, most children are vaccinated, and infant mortality rates are low. The population bomb has fizzled, and human numbers are stabilizing and even declining in many parts of the world. Health care is improving and communicable diseases are receding even as the threat of pandemics remains. Our technological capacity to solve problems is accelerating. Life is good and getting better for billions of people.[1] These positive trends can continue.

But Earth's climate is changing. National governments are paralyzed by tribal politics. Water tables are dropping. Unequal opportunity is disrupting politics. Species are going extinct. Rural to urban migration is overwhelming city infrastructure. People remain trapped in poverty. Agricultural productivity is not keeping up with demand. Resource scarcities are creating price volatility and disrupting supply chains. Approaches to solving problems are piecemeal, stalled, anachronistic, and corrupt.

This book unpacks these characteristics of the Anthropocene, in chapter 2, because they present humanity's greatest challenges and opportunities. Two narratives dominate most presentations of the Anthropocene: decline and breakthrough. We emphasize breakthrough because it invites collaboration, innovation, and action (rather than fear, despair, and helplessness). It is easy to be overwhelmed by the challenges, but we want to make sure you see the opportunities.

The declinist narrative is popular among some environmentalists and news outlets trying to capture attention with fear-filled headlines. It is a story of population explosion, finite Earth, species extinctions, ecological degradation, social decline, pandemics, and related catastrophes that are supposed to be inevitable if we don't reverse course and head back to more natural, communal, traditional conditions. The breakthrough narrative, in contrast, looks forward rather than backward. It suggests we can sustain development, improve social and environmental conditions, and, if we are so inclined, create a new Eden. It is optimistic and hopeful but not naive.

The breakthrough narrative clearly recognizes that business-as-usual is unsustainable. Human civilization will crash and burn if we don't overcome the challenges discussed throughout this book: climate change, agricultural expansion, urbanization, inequality, finite resources and a linear economy, and so on. But the breakthrough narrative suggests that if we address these challenges, bend our development trajectory a bit, sacrifice a little here, and innovate a bit there, then we can construct a future that is prosperous, healthy, wise, tolerant, beautiful, or whatever future conditions we decide to create (the United Nations' Sustainable Development Goals describe one version of a desired future, but there are many others to choose from or co-create).

This breakthrough storyline invites people to join in creating their future rather than turning back, or retreating, into a declinist perspective of fatalistic doom and gloom. It is a story that invites broad participation by business, government, and civil society. It invites people like you to play an active role in engaging, navigating, and innovating the future. It demands leadership from you and many others, leading from where you are to adjust and transform humanity's development trajectory, so we overcome challenges and turn them into opportunities. The Anthropocene is a heady time, especially for environmental and sustainability professionals. This is your opportunity, and challenge, to provide leadership and influence as never before.

Leadership

It is almost clichéd to say this, but environmental problems are people problems. Overcoming them requires more than science and technology; it requires leadership. So, then, what is leadership?

Leadership, as explained in chapter 4, is the creation of three conditions: *direction*, *alignment*, and *commitment*. These conditions exist pretty much any time and any place a group of people manages to get things done: people agree on the direction that defines what they want to achieve, align their efforts and resources to achieve that direction, and commit to helping each other and maintaining the work over time.

Importantly, this conception of leadership places responsibility for leadership on the shoulders of stakeholders. All stakeholders—not just the few designated leaders with titles, corner offices, and elected positions—can, and should, practice leadership to make direction, alignment, and commitment happen. Stated differently, leadership is something everyone can do, not just people in positions of formal authority. Everyone can and should lead from where they are. In fact, we will argue that the only way leadership can happen in wicked situations is if stakeholders co-construct direction, alignment, and commitment. Hopefully, you find this conception of leadership empowering. We do, and that is why we wrote this book, to help you apply wicked leadership skills and practices to wicked situations.

Transforming Careers

Your influence and relevance depend, in part, on being in the right place at the right time. You risk being left behind or swept away if you don't see the challenges and opportunities coming your way. The Anthropocene is causing tectonic transformations in markets and governance systems (especially businesses and cities). The emerging landscape is reshaping organizations, professions, and careers—that is, creating new opportunities for influence and relevance. This book explores these changes and the impacts they are having on careers and opportunities, specifically in markets, cities, and governance.

- Markets: Capitalist markets may be the most powerful force of change on Earth. Sustainability concerns about the Anthropocene are transforming markets. Forward-thinking businesses already integrate sustainability concerns into their core management practices, including operational efficiency, capital acquisition, strategic direction, risk management, human resources, and market growth.

- Cities: Most people live in cities, most wealth is in cities, and people continue to move to cities. Cities have the motivation, expertise, and resources to fundamentally transform how society meets its material needs and sustains development. Cities are innovating and acting because they must and they can. Cities are often the primary incubators for novel solutions to Anthropocene challenges, especially when nation-states are unable or unwilling to act.

- Governance: Anthropocenic challenges and opportunities exceed the respective capacities of governments, businesses, and civil society. Cross-sector collaboration is required. Thus new models of governance are emerging with novel functions and processes for a wide range of stakeholders, including environmental and sustainability professionals.

Book Outline

The book has three parts: a roadmap, a toolbox, and a storybook.

The roadmap part of the book helps navigate the opportunities and challenges that the Anthropocene creates for you and your profession, career, and community (Table 1.1). Chapter 2 introduces the Anthropocene. It explains the breakthrough narrative presented earlier and the daunting challenges we face, including ending carbon pollution, adapting to climate change, making supply chains resilient, transitioning from poverty to prosperity, and educating and empowering vulnerable populations. Chapter 3 helps you consider your own responses to the Anthropocene. It reviews how and why key transformations are occurring in business, cities, and governance, and how to position yourself to have influence and relevance now and in the future.

Table 1.1. Roadmap for the Anthropocene

Wicked Anthropocene challenges (Chapter 2)	Diverse stakeholders (Chapter 3 and case studies)
• Climate change	• Professionals
• Water Risk	• Experts
• Agriculture and food	• Businesses
• Urbanization	• Governments
• Population	• Cities
• Poverty	• NGOs
• Inequality	• Communities
• Prosperity	• Citizens
• Biodiversity	• Consumers
• Energy	
• Linear economy	

The toolbox part of the book drills down into specific leadership skills, practices, and principles for addressing the wicked challenges of the Anthropocene (Table 1.2). Chapter 4 defines wickedness and introduces leadership as a response to it. It explains the Direction–Alignment–Commitment leadership theory and explains why leading from where you are is both possible and necessary. It differentiates this leadership theory from competing leadership theories. Chapters 5, 6, and 7 present specific leadership practices designed for different aspects of wicked situations. Chapter 5 focuses on connecting and coordinating action among widely dispersed stakeholders who may never meet nor know they are related; that is, they are actors from different organizations, sectors, and regions. Chapter 6 focuses on collaborating across values and identities that divide, polarize, and paralyze stakeholders. Chapter 7 focuses on adapting to change and working with confounding uncertainty, including learning by doing, sharing lessons, and building capacity to fail forward.

The third part of the book tells real stories about sustainability professionals leading from where they are, and applying leadership skills

Table 1.2. Leadership Toolbox: Wicked Leadership Practices

Connect (chapter 5)	Collaborate (chapter 6)	Adapt (chapter 7)
Accountability	Manage filter bubbles and echo chambers	Sensemaking
Story telling	Pick battles	Learn by failing
Community of practice	Emphasize identity not facts	Innovation
Train-the-trainer	Boundary spanning	Sharing lessons
Scaling-up	Trust	Be disruptive
Diffusion	Conflict management	Resiliency not efficiency
Collective impact	Partner	Scenario planning
Information campaigns		

and practices to the challenges and opportunities of the Anthropocene (Table 1.3). These stories not only illustrate wicked leadership tools but will also inspire and empower you to use them to do something similar in your own work, and hopefully improve upon them. Chapters 8 through 15 profile the actions of people from multiple sectors, including business, government, and civil society organizations. In these stories, you will learn about people like you leading from where they are, embracing opportunities and tackling challenges of the Anthropocene head-on.

Table 1.3. Leadership Storybook

Case studies of leadership for sustainability

- Chapter 9: Diet, meat, and sustainable food systems
- Chapter 10: Water, sanitation, health, and women empowerment
- Chapter 11: Cities and climate change
- Chapter 12: Farming, innovation, and climate mitigation
- Chapter 13: Sustainable investing: business risk and profit
- Chapter 14: Biodiversity, fire, and learning networks
- Chapter 15: Partnering for clean water and community benefit

Imagine

Imagine a future in which energy is cheap, safe, clean, abundant, and sourced from ocean tides, solar panels, wind turbines, next-generation nuclear power, and smart buildings that feed energy back into the grid. Imagine a future where ample, healthy food comes from restored land, cultured bacteria, and alternatives to livestock. Imagine a future where biodiversity flourishes because farms increase productivity so much that half of the land devoted to agriculture has been retired and reverted to forest and habitat. Imagine a future where water is not scarce because municipalities and buildings capture and recycle wastewater. Imagine a future with less traffic because vehicles become shared, autonomous, and electric. Imagine a future where most people live in smart, dense, walkable, safe, healthy, mixed-use cities full of plazas and parks.

Imagine a future in which human population has stabilized at six billion healthy, wealthy, and educated individuals living in peaceful communities connected by sustainable supply chains. Imagine a future where most electronics, automobiles, appliances, and other durable products are engineered to be rented, not bought, from socially responsible businesses committed to maintaining them and reusing the finite materials they contain in a circular economy. Imagine a future without poverty and hunger, with education for all, and average salaries, globally, of at least $100,000 (in today's dollars), made possible by global trade, fully functioning institutions, and a robust rule of law.

Imagine how you would orient your career, community, business, and government if this future were reachable within 100 years. Imagine how you can help create this future. Imagine that the technology to get there exists, and that what we lack is leadership. Imagine that wicked leadership skills bring these solutions within reach. Imagine what you can do with a book about wicked leadership.

PART I

Roadmap for the Anthropocene

CHAPTER 2

Challenges of the Anthropocene

In the beginning, according to the scientific creation story, Earth formed about five billion years ago. At first, only physical forces—gravity, heat, climate, and chemistry—shaped the planet. Then, after about one billion years, replicating life emerged. Evolution became another global change agent, accelerating erosion; oxygenating the atmosphere; creating soil, oil, and limestone; and changing the climate. Just recently, in a blink of geological and evolutionary time, another global change agent emerged with enough power and creativity to remake Earth: humanity.

Humans differentiated from the other great apes about five million years ago. Modern humans, *Homo sapiens*, anatomically and genetically similar to the authors and readers of this book, appeared on the scene a couple hundred thousand years ago. Sapiens migrated to all parts of Earth, outcompeting and outbreeding other human species who evolved and migrated out of Africa before us. For most of our time on Earth, we were insignificant actors in Earth's history, living hunter–gatherer lifestyles not too different from those of our many evolutionary cousins.

Things changed rapidly during the last 12,000 years—what geologists call the Holocene—a time of relatively stable and nurturing environmental conditions that provided an incubation period for human culture and modern civilization. Agriculture took root 10,000 years ago and changed climate and biodiversity. Cities, specialization of labor, trade, and markets soon followed. Written language and math began 5,000 years ago. Pivotal prophets and teachers—Buddha, Confucius, Jesus, Moses, Muhammad, Plato—all taught and preached within the last 3,500 years. Countries—modern nation-states that dominate contemporary global and regional politics—emerged only 500 years ago. Capitalism, democracy, corporations, fossil fuels, and the Industrial Revolution are even more recent innovations. Virtually all the technology and culture upon which humans now rely was developed in less than five hundred human generations, and all during the stable and nurturing Holocene.

Volatile change and increasing uncertainty are replacing the stable and nurturing environmental conditions of the Holocene. Figure 2.1 shows the accelerating changes that characterize recent history. The trends are stark and startling. Starting around 1950, just about every social and environmental indicator arcs upward. These graphs are not based on predictions or models: they are plots of actual data, changes that have already occurred. Basically, humanity is remaking its nest; we are fundamentally reordering our life support systems. Some call this new era the Anthropocene: "anthropo" refers to humans, "cene" refers to geological time. The Anthropocene is the time of human responsibility for Earth's conditions.[1]

Changing conditions present new challenges and opportunities. In the past, even mild disruptions of climate and other environmental conditions wreaked havoc on humanity, causing famine, disease, war, and even the end of civilizations.[2] Accelerating changes during the Anthropocene could prove much more disruptive and demand new ways to provide the safety, comfort, goods, and services modern human civilization requires.

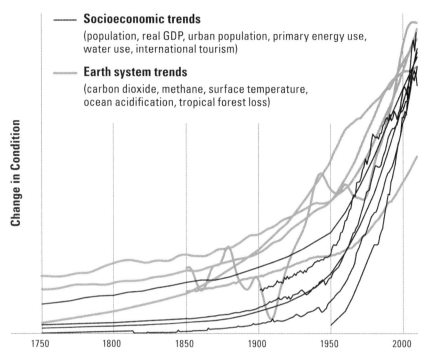

Figure 2.1. Changes to environmental and social conditions have been accelerating dramatically, creating novel challenges for human civilization. (The figure is based on Will Steffen, Wendy Broadgate, Lisa Deutsch, Owen Gaffney, and Cornelia Ludwig, "The Trajectory of the Anthropocene: The Great Acceleration," *The Anthropocene Review* 2, no. 1 [2015]: 81–98.)

The Anthropocene changes the narrative. Humanity becomes the key actor; not gods, evolution, or geology. Humans create Earth's conditions that support or threaten civilization. Humans decide whether to become wealthier, healthier, better connected, better educated, and more innovative or drive off the cliff of ecological collapse. Fortunately, we humans possess the ability to take stock of who we are, what roles we play in shaping Earth's history, and where our story is going. The next section addresses several key challenges that leadership practices must navigate.

Breaking Through to Sustainable Development

It is impossible to predict the future, and no attempt is made to do so here, but it is increasingly clear that things are changing and that change is accelerating. Some of those changes, if they continue, will present existential challenges for human civilization. Thus business as usual appears unsustainable. The outlines of key challenges become clearer and closer every day. They are the rocks upon which our development trajectory will founder, the whirlpools that will capsize civilization, and the bottleneck that stifles progress (Figure 2.2). We probably have only a few decades, maybe fifty years, before one or more of these challenges disrupt our development options, resulting in a great deal of

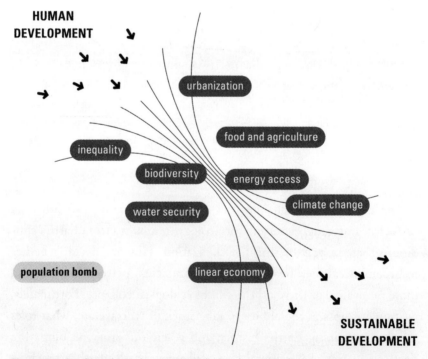

Figure 2.2. Breaking through to sustainable development. Challenges converging over the next fifty years have the potential to disrupt civilization.

human suffering, environmental harm, and lost opportunity. We need to navigate, innovate, intervene, engage, influence, and change these challenges into opportunities.

On the other side of this metaphorical bottleneck, people are more prosperous, educated, and healthy than they are today; the economy is circular; pollution and waste are minimal; clean energy and water are abundant; climate has stabilized at adaptable conditions; most people reside in livable cities; and ample habitat exists for biodiversity and ecosystems to flourish.[3] That future, no doubt, will have its own set of challenges; but to get there, we must first navigate the challenges we can see. We have the technology to do so. All we need is leadership.

Here we briefly review a few of the most obvious and immediate challenges: population, prosperity, urbanization, food, water, climate/energy, linear economy, and inequality. As discussed in the next chapter, responses to these challenges by markets and governance are reshaping professions and careers, so the better you understand the challenges, the better positioned you will be to become relevant and influential.

Population

Good news! We are successfully navigating one challenge—the population bomb.[4] Human population exploded during a short 200-year window: almost one billion by 1800, two billion in 1930, four billion in 1974, over seven billion today, and perhaps adding several billion more by the end of this century. At first blush, these statistics make it tempting to frame population growth as the key challenge to sustainable development. This framing would be a mistake. A key theme of the Anthropocene story told in this book—and something many dyed-in-the-wool environmentalists will resist—is to move beyond framing population as the problem. That framing is troublesome for several reasons. First, it is not accurate. As will be discussed in this chapter, the demographic transition is leading to population decline, not explosion, and decline might pose a bigger challenge for sustainable development. Second, the population bomb framing puts sustainability professionals in the politically unwinnable position of arguing that babies are bad. It makes us appear misanthropic, shrill, and uncaring about one of the most basic human rights—being a parent. Third, the real problem is prosperity: meeting the needs of billions of wealthier people. Prosperity is a good problem to have because it means we can reduce poverty, illiteracy, and malnutrition, and benefit from the creativity and productivity of a growing global middle class.

Currently, the number of humans is increasing in absolute terms, but the rate of increase is slowing every year and will eventually level off and decline. We've nearly reached "peak child" (Figure 2.3). The number of children in the world will continue to grow a bit more over the next decade or so, perhaps until 2050, but then there will never be more children alive than at that moment in time—perhaps a turning point we will memorialize. At some point in the 2020s, for the first time in human history, the number of people over the age of 65 will be greater than the number under the age of 5. By 2050, the number of those over 65 should exceed those under 14.

Demographers call this trend the demographic transition. Parents birth fewer babies for several reasons. First, improved health care reduces child mortality, meaning parents aren't faced with the horrible dilemma of birthing many children hoping a few will survive. Second, increasing wealth and a retirement safety net mean parents need not rely on children to support them during old age. Third, agriculture has been mechanized, fewer people live on farms, and children are not needed for farm labor. Instead, most families live and work in urban areas, where children are expensive to feed and house. Fourth, and perhaps most importantly, the number of children per family declines as women become more educated, empowered to make choices beyond or besides motherhood (i.e.,

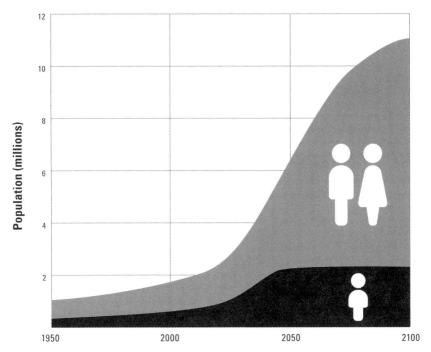

Figure 2.3. Peak child and the demographic transition. Changes in reproduction rate are leading to the decline and stabilization of the human population. (Adapted from M. Roser "When Will the World Reach 'Peak Child?'" Our World in Data, February 8, 2018, https://ourworldindata.org/peak-child.)

empowered to be more than mothers), and gain access to birth control. Today, population growth rates are actually below replacement (i.e., less than 2.1) in relatively wealthy countries where women have rights equal to men, and where good health care and retirement safety nets exist. The United Nations reports that forty-eight countries are expected to have shrinking populations between now and 2050 due to falling fertility rates, outmigration, and high mortality. Greece's population started to decline in 2011. Fewer babies were born in Italy in 2015 than in any year since the state was formed, and in that same year, 200 schools closed across Poland for lack of children. Portugal could lose up to half its population by 2060. These trends are occurring throughout Europe and other developed countries. China and many Asian countries are not far behind: China may face having 600 million fewer citizens by 2100.

What will happen to our social structures, politics, and economy when our population declines and ages? Consider some of the implications.[5] Declining birth rates will produce fewer consumers, as well as fewer and older workers. Innovation may decline as our population ages because much of today's innovation comes from young people. Fewer and older people in the workforce also means tax collections decline, hindering government functions; but the need for schools, roads, bridges, dams, and airports may also decline, while health care costs will rise.

This section should not be interpreted as suggesting that human population growth is unimportant or that the global trends are evenly distributed (e.g., populations in developing regions of Africa are still growing very rapidly and will for some time). Rather, the main message is this: human population growth is no longer an obstacle to sustainable development, and perhaps it never was, despite the incendiary metaphors of "bomb" and "explosion" embedded in much environmental discourse. Yes, absolutely, we should continue the important work of family planning, empowering women, reducing infant mortality, supporting safety nets, and other factors that hasten the demographic transition. There is much work of this type left to be done, and the people and programs that do this good work are necessary and important. Fortunately, they are succeeding: we are navigating this challenge, and some countries have turned their attention to navigating depopulation.

Prosperity, more so than population, is a major challenge of the Anthropocene. And that is a good challenge to have.

Prosperity

September 2018 marked a global tipping point, when more than 50 percent of the world's population lived in households with enough discretionary expenditure to be considered "middle class" or "rich." For the first time ever, the poor and vulnerable were no longer the global majority. Today, about five people per second are entering the middle class. The number of rich are increasing too (one person every two seconds). Barring some global economic setback, we have entered a new era of a middle-class majority.[6]

Most of the growth in prosperity will happen in Asia and Africa. By 2050, middle class consumption in Brazil, China, India, Indonesia, Vietnam, and other currently "emerging" economies could be larger than the economies of G7 nations that dominated the post-WWII global economy (Canada, France, Germany, Italy, Japan, the United Kingdom, and the United States). While people in developed nations such as the US tend to be pessimistic about the state of their own middle classes, the rest of the world—the approximately 90 percent of global citizens who live outside the West—are instead saying, "We have never had better times."[7]

The size of the global economy provides one indicator of prosperity. In the year AD 1, the global economy totaled less than 20 billion US dollars (in today's dollars). The economy was not quite ten times that amount 1,800 years later: $175 billion. But then, with the help of the Industrial Revolution, fossil fuels, capitalism, and global trade, the economy grew exponentially, exceeding $41 trillion by 2000. Predictions of future growth suggest several more doublings this century. To put that in perspective, a global average annual income approaching $100,000 per person (in today's dollars) is possible by the year 2100.[8] Poverty, meanwhile, has been declining for several centuries and is near its lowest level ever.

Other indicators of improved prosperity include health, education, and other conditions of social progress, such as the capacities to solve problems, govern ourselves, increase security, and build safety nets to catch people that fall off the economic ladder. Nobel Prize winner

Angus Deaton's recent book, *The Great Escape*, chronicles humanity's remarkable escape from poverty, subsistence, malnutrition, and illness. The introduction begins, "Life is better now than at almost any time in history." Similar arguments have been made by Hans Rosling in *Factfulness*. Steven Pinker, in *Angels of Our Better Nature*, documents the rise of peace and safety and the decline of violence and war, and in *Enlightenment Now*, Pinker documents trends of rising prosperity, health, education, quality of life, and happiness. The accessible website *Our World in Data* presents similar data. Several trends that lend themselves to numbers are summarized in Table 2.1.

Table 2.1. Accelerating Prosperity

Year (AD)	Percent Literacy	Percent Child mortality	Percent Vaccinated	Total world economy (billions)	Average annual per person income
1800	12	43	0	175	194
1900	21	36	0	1,100	667
2000	82	8	82	41,000	6,721
2100	98	unknown	unknown	300,000–1,000,000	100,000

Literacy and child mortality data from World in Data. Total world economy estimates based on work by economic historian J. B. DeLong reported in https://en.wikipedia.org/wiki/Gross_world_product. Average annual income assumes wealth is equally divided. Predictions for 2100 are based on scenarios developed for the Intergovernmental Panel on Climate Change described in chapter 7 of this book in the section on scenario planning. Monetary units are US dollars and adjusted for inflation.

As a result of spreading prosperity, people who once focused only on day-to-day survival and security now demand other basics of modern life—education, health care, information, travel, and leisure. They can focus on longer-term concerns: their children's opportunities, their community's good governance, their career, their material well-being, and the meaning of life. They also become able to engage the global economy by purchasing washing machines, motorized transportation, furnishings, meat, and more. This new consumption in turn accelerates environmental and social changes, creating the Anthropocene and many of the challenges we face.

To sum up the message so far: prosperity, not population, is the key driver of the challenges we face in the coming decades and century. This is a good problem to have because we want more people to be more empowered, healthy, educated, and secure.

Urbanization

Humanity will build, in the next few decades, more roads, buildings, pipes, sewage treatment plants, and other urban infrastructure than was built over the entirety of civilization, investing perhaps $6 trillion per year. Pause and ponder the resources required. Each year, the world now uses more steel than it used in the entire decade after World War II and more cement than it used during the first half of the twentieth century. Mind-boggling statistics about China's urbanization provide a specific illustration: China is the most rapidly urbanizing country in history. Each year for the last decade, more than twenty million Chinese relocated to cities, which is more people than currently live in downtown New York City, Los Angeles, and Chicago combined. Other rapidly urbanizing nations are not far behind, perhaps none more consequential than India.

The cause of all this development? Rural to urban migration. People have been moving to urban areas for centuries in search of jobs, education, equal rights, health care, entertainment, partners, and urban amenities. In 1800, only 10 percent of people lived in urban areas. That doubled by 1900 and more than doubled again by 2000. Projections suggest that by 2050, nearly 70 percent of people will live in urban areas. This trend means that between now and 2050 we will add approximately two billion new people to city spaces that have yet to be built—probably more than one million people a week. Cities with over ten million people—so-called megacities—increased from ten in 1990 to twenty-three in 2010. By 2030 there could be forty, and perhaps more than a billion people will live in megacities.

The social disruption caused by urbanization may be more challenging than the environmental impacts. In North America and Europe, during the late 1800s and early 1900s, poor, rural, displaced farm labor migrated to cities seeking employment and opportunity. They were poorly housed and easily exploited, and they worked in unsafe conditions. Eventually, and often disruptively, these workers transformed into a politically and economically powerful urban middle class. Urbanization in today's developing countries is driven by the same decline of rural agricultural economies but punctuated by spurts of mass migration escaping civil, natural, or climate-caused disasters. The scale and rapidity of migration are overwhelming urban infrastructure and disrupting social functions. Many cities in developing countries are stretched to the breaking point, with perhaps a billion people struggling to survive in urban slums.[9] Threats of contagion, such as with COVID-19, poise enormous challenges for mass transit, a technology upon which sustainable urban development depends.

Fortunately, as discussed in the next chapter, when done well, urbanization fuels economic growth, pulls people out of poverty, increases human rights, and reduces per person environmental impacts. For this reason, it may be one of the most important trends promoting sustainable development. Despite the coronavirus pandemic and other troubling trends,[10] cities, particularly outside the developed world, remain powerful forces for development, and their growth seems likely to continue.

Food and Agriculture

The invention of agriculture tamed and expanded the food supply, giving rise to population growth, permanent settlements, and a leisure class. Modern agriculture enables a relatively few people to produce reliable, safe, abundant food for the rest of us; freeing us to create cities, businesses, art, governments, universities, cathedrals, science, and literature. But agriculture also comes with some costs: it disrupts how and where people live, and it damages Earth's ecosystems, perhaps more so than anything else humans do.

The statistics paint a stark picture: agriculture uses 70 percent of freshwater supplies and emits 30 percent of greenhouse gases.[11] If cattle were able to form their own nation, they would rank as the third-largest greenhouse gas emitter, just behind the Chinese and Americans. Humanity has already converted most of Earth's forests and grasslands to farms, an area roughly the size of two continents—South America and Africa—combined, causing species to go extinct because of lost habitat. We now capture and use more nitrogen than all nonhuman parts of the biosphere combined, and we use most of it to fertilize agriculture (nitrogen fertilizer boosts crop growth and is responsible for almost half our food). But nitrogen has harmful impacts. Nitrous oxide disrupts the ozone layer, which protects us from cancer-causing radiation. It is also a powerful greenhouse gas and is thus a major contributor to climate change. It washes off farms into our rivers and bays, causing algae eruptions that, when the algae die and decay, choke off oxygen, kill fish, and excrete toxic wastes. These so-called dead zones exist around the world, over a total area greater than ten New Jerseys.

As the foregoing statistics indicate, we are already hammering the biosphere to produce the food we currently consume. Yet demand for food is projected to increase dramatically. Some of that food will feed the two billion additional people expected to join us between now and 2050. But the greatest increase in demand for food will be driven by rising prosperity. Wealthier people tend to prefer higher-calorie, meatier diets. More meat eating may be the biggest food challenge because meat production is so inefficient: meat-based protein takes many more barrels of oil, liters of water, and hectares of land to produce the same nutritional value as provided by plants.

These challenges are huge and growing. Innovative solutions include changing diets, reducing waste, designing new foods, and using information technology to make agriculture more precise and effective. Their implementation will require wicked leadership. Chapter 9 contains a leadership story about changing diets away from meat.

Water

Clean, accessible, reliable water is, arguably, a human right.[12] Yet almost 1.5 million children die every year from diseases caused by unclean water: 4,000 deaths a day, or one every twenty seconds. Roughly one in eight people do not have adequate access to safe drinking water, and almost two in five don't have access to adequate sanitation. They must carry water into their homes, which requires so much time and effort that someone in the household, most likely a female, will skip school and forgo other opportunities, including the many benefits that flow from education. According to one telling statistic, females in sub-Saharan Africa spend forty billion hours a year collecting water: that is equivalent to a year's worth of labor by the entire workforce in France. We can do better.

Water tables around the world are dropping as we pump water faster than aquifers can replenish: about six feet a year in Mexico, ten feet a year in Iran, and perhaps even more in India and China. Once the water is withdrawn, subsidence from soil compaction often follows. The photo shows one of the most famous examples in the US, identified by Dr. Joseph F. Poland (Figure 2.4). Signs on the pole indicate the land surface elevation in 1925, 1955, and 1977. The site is in the San Joaquin Valley southwest of Mendota, California, and home to important agricultural production.

Figure 2.4. California land subsidence. Changes in land elevation due to depleting groundwater in order to irrigate crops. (Photo credit: Dr. Joseph F. Poland, USGS.)

Coastal cities are particularly impacted because lower elevations caused by subsidence combine with rising sea levels from climate change to accelerate and accentuate flooding. Dramatic examples abound. Jakarta, the capital of Indonesia, has sunk almost two meters. Now half of it is below current sea level, and many of these areas must be abandoned, making Jakarta one of the most rapidly shrinking cities in the world, despite being a megacity of ten million. As a result, plans are under way to abandon Jakarta as the national capital and relocate to a new location on the island of Borneo.

Since drilling and pumping began in the Ogallala Aquifer, perhaps the most important aquifer for agriculture in the United States, water has retreated more than one hundred feet, and concerns about depleting the aquifer that irrigates America's breadbasket seem well founded. Saudi Arabia stopped growing wheat because it drained so much water out of its aquifers that ancient springs and oases went dry. Many countries, short on water, now import virtual water by importing food and other water-intensive products. Problematically, many countries that are short on water are also exporting virtual water, often in the form of agricultural goods. We are only just beginning to understand the implications of this burgeoning global trade in virtual water.[13]

Let's dig a bit deeper into the rising demand for water. We use perhaps 70 percent of all freshwater to grow our food, mostly to irrigate crops. Recall that demand for food will increase dramatically in the coming decades. Our energy system uses another 10 to 20 percent of our freshwater to spin turbines, liquefy tar sands, wash coal, cool boilers, and so on. And, as discussed in the next section, demand for energy is expected to increase as well. Industries and municipalities combine to use the remaining 10 to 20 percent of freshwater (the amount varies by region). Fortunately, water use is declining in many developed cities because of building codes and other policies that require improved technologies, such as low-water-intensity manufacturing, low-flow showers, efficient washing machines, xeriscape lawns, and repairs of leaky infrastructure.[14]

Most multinational businesses already regard water risk as a key constraint to growth and profits, with fiscal impacts already in the billions.[15] These impacts will likely be exacerbated by climate change and could cost some regions up to 6 percent of their GDP, spur out-migration, and spark political conflict. In the US, many counties in key agricultural regions are projected to experience severe water risk by 2050. Navigating the growing conflict and uncertainty will require effective leadership. Chapter 10 presents a leadership story about a poor, rural, Indian community improving its water access.

Energy and Climate

Civilization depends on affordable, abundant energy to fertilize and irrigate agriculture; power cars and computers; air condition and illuminate buildings; and manufacture materials like cement, steel, and silica. Our switch to fossil fuels slowed deforestation because fewer trees were cut for fuel, saved the world's whales and seals from being harvested for their oil, and, by intensifying agricultural production, halved the amount of land needed to produce a given amount of food.[16] Accessible, reliable, safe, affordable energy literally and figuratively pulls people out of poverty. It is arguably a human right. As stated by United Nations Secretary General Ban Ki-moon, "Energy is the golden thread that connects economic growth, increased social equity, and an environment that allows the world to thrive." Yet over a billion people still lack access to electricity. Perhaps two billion must burn solid biomass (e.g., wood, grass, dung) to heat and cook, suffering respiratory ailments because they inhale particulate matter and forgoing education and economic opportunity because they must spend time foraging for energy. As prosperity spreads and people climb out of poverty and into the more energy-intensive lifestyles of the global middle class, global energy consumption will grow, perhaps 30 percent by 2050.[17]

But even without increasing energy production to meet the emerging demand, our carbon-centric energy system threatens our health with toxins released into air and water. It threatens regional economies with disasters such as the Deepwater Horizon oil spills in the Gulf of Mexico. It threatens biodiversity because huge swaths of habitat get scraped off, boiled, drilled, and destroyed during fuel extraction. And, most ominously, it threatens our climate because burning fossil fuels emits greenhouse gases that cause global warming. So we face a daunting challenge: more energy is needed today to lift billions out of poverty; more energy will be needed tomorrow to meet the needs of several billion new middle-class consumers; and current energy production already poses grave threats. Wind, solar, geothermal, tidal, nuclear, and other carbon-lite sources of energy are expanding rapidly, but barely fast enough to keep up with new demand, let alone to replace existing energy production.[18]

Let's drill down a bit further into the conundrum of climate change. Adapting to more than 2 degrees of warming may be manageable, but it will likely be very costly and produce massive hardships. The disruptions caused by 4 to 6 degrees of warming will change civilization as we know it. Our "carbon budget" is the amount of carbon gases we can emit and stay below 2-degree warming.[19] We are on course to exceed that budget, even if countries meet their public pledges to reduce emissions. We have already purchased and installed enough carbon-emitting devices—automobile gas tanks, water heaters, coal- or gas-powered electrical generators, and so on—to emit almost 80 percent of that budget. It will be financially and politically difficult to retire and replace these carbon-emitting investments before they are paid off and reach the end of their productive lives. So, unless we find the political will (and funding) to retire those carbon emitters early, we are nearly 80 percent on our way to 2 degrees of warming. Plus, as already noted, we need to produce a whole lot more energy to meet the basic needs of many and the rising desires of the growing middle class. Chapter 11 presents a leadership story about a city dramatically reducing its greenhouse gas emissions.

Linear Economy

Our economy is a marvel of productivity and efficiency. It provides most of us with the food, shelter, and other necessities we need to survive, and some of us with luxuries we crave. Moreover, continued economic growth promises to end poverty and malnutrition, this century, and welcome billions more into the middle class. But the linear design of our economy—in which goods are manufactured from raw materials, used, and then discarded as waste—depletes natural resources and eventually, ultimately, is unsustainable on a finite planet. As the UN Environment Programme's Green Economy Initiative has reported, "Achieving sustainability rests almost entirely on getting the economy right." And getting the economy right requires reforming the linear economy into something more circular; without this reform, our means of production and consumption become obstacles to sustainable development.

Finite materials are not the obstacle to sustainable development; the linear economy is. This assertion is important and often misunderstood. Sustainability advocates can get stuck in the Malthusian, finite-Earth, carrying-capacity paradigm, which argues that we are running out of materials. The circular economy paradigm acknowledges that Earth's resources are finite, but it contends that finite resources are not a limitation to continued economic growth because, given enough ingenuity and energy, we can continuously reuse most materials and get the balance of our material needs from renewable sources.

Thus far in human history, our linear economy has not been much constrained by resource availability. Resource consumption, having increased by 50 percent from 1980 to 2000 and by 75 percent from 2000 to 2015, is on pace to double over the next decade.[20] Even with all this consumption and disposal of natural resources, the relative cost of supplying new resources declined, which means innovation, efficiency, and resource discoveries increased or replaced the supply of resources at a rate that kept up with and exceeded the fast-growing demand.

But this situation might be changing. Resource shortages and supply disruptions now cause troubling price volatility, which creates business risks that affect profit margins.[21] A circular economy can address this, while creating astounding opportunities; many trillions of dollars will be made by those who innovate first. The challenges, however, are huge because it requires transforming capitalist markets—perhaps humanity's largest institution. Fortunately, many individuals and organizations are focusing on the development of circular economic systems. This market transformation is discussed in detail in chapter 3 because it creates unique opportunities for professionals to position their careers for influence and relevance.

Inequality

Good news:[22] statistics show a narrowing gap between the economies of emerging and developed countries. Over the last thirty years, the developing nations have urbanized, industrialized, and increased global trading, and they are catching up, economically, with wealthier countries. From this vantage point, inequality is declining.

Bad news:[23] while most everyone's income and material lifestyle have been improving, the gap between the bottom and top has been widening. Within-country inequality, which declined globally for much of the twentieth century, began increasing in the 1980s. Most people alive today are witnessing larger income disparities than their parents did. Levels of income inequality in the two largest economies in the world—the US and China—are at or near their historic peaks. Globally, the top 1 percent of the population now controls about 50 percent of the world's wealth. The employment picture also looks bleak: the risk of holding a low-paying, insecure job is higher today than in 1995, and

40 percent of the world's employable youth are either unemployed or working but still living in poverty.

Inequality triggers several feedback loops that negatively impact sustainable development.[24] It slows economic growth by reducing consumer demand because people don't have money to spend. It decreases worker productivity because people can't access housing, education, and health care. It shortens periods of economic growth because many households lack savings and resources to weather small setbacks. The resulting economic instability harms the institutions that support worker health and education because these institutions receive fewer long-term investments, which, in turn, creates another feedback loop, accelerating inequality as workers at the margins become less healthy, less educated, and less economically productive. Inequality also threatens political stability and security. Economic history teaches us that when economic growth slows, political tensions escalate, and the haves become less willing to share with the have-nots, creating another positive feedback loop of reduced public investment, increasing inequality while further reducing economic growth. Further, inequality limits the voice and political influence of the disadvantaged because it concentrates wealth and political power. Those with limited political voice risk losing respect and the protection of their rights, which in turn fosters distrust, increases social tensions and conflict, and weakens social capital.

The resulting social justice and security concerns may threaten sustainable development at local to global scales. Increasing the number of people with few prospects for employment, health care, hope, marriage, social mobility, or geographic migration creates a recipe for social unrest.

Conclusion

This chapter tells a story about a transition from a stable and nurturing Holocene to a dynamic and uncertain Anthropocene. It is a story that asks humanity to navigate great risks and realize even greater opportunities. Despite the enormous challenges we face, sustainable development is within reach. We already see opportunities emerging out of these challenges. After 2100, the human population may level off at six to eight billion people (maybe less) who are healthy, well fed, prosperous, mostly urban, and living in a thriving biosphere supportive of human civilization. Addressing the climate change challenge could produce clean energy and employment opportunities. Increasing agricultural productivity may increase wildlife habitat and ecosystem services as marginal farms revert to forest. Narrowing inequality can boost productivity and inventiveness. A circular economy could change brittle supply chains into resilient value nets. There is hope for our future and much work to do.

Chapter 3 examines the tectonic transformation in markets and governance currently unfolding as our institutions respond to the Anthropocene. It will help you position yourself to have greater influence and relevance as your profession, organization, and community change.

CHAPTER 3

Opportunities of the Anthropocene

Your influence and relevance depend, in part, on being in the right place at the right time. You risk being left behind or swept away if you don't see opportunities and risks coming your way.

Attention: Opportunities and risks are coming your way! The Great Acceleration and Anthropocene challenges are transforming markets, governance, and governments. This chapter helps you understand how these changes impact your organization, community, profession, and career.

Careers addressing sustainability challenges and opportunities are increasingly common. The International Labor Organization, in *World Employment and Social Outlook*, estimates twenty-four million "green" jobs will be created by 2030. *Forbes* magazine notes that corporate executive management teams increasingly include positions focusing on sustainability and social responsibility, which means these issues receive more attention and more staff and budgets. According to the *GreenBiz State of the Profession* report, there has been a mainstreaming or "professionalization" of sustainability in traditional roles in most organizations. Public administration, engineering, accounting, business management, public relations, architecture, and urban planning, for example, increasingly incorporate sustainability principles, tools, and responsibilities in their formal training and job descriptions. Lisa Shpritz, environmental business and engagement executive at Bank of America, speaking at the 2019 Climate Leadership Conference in Baltimore, recommended that people looking for work in this field should not just look for jobs with "sustainability" in the title. Rather, she suggests, "You can do sustainability from any job." Also—and importantly for readers—employees using their sustainability skills earn higher salaries![1]

Professional societies and credentialing organizations support the growing ranks of sustainability professionals by offering training and networks to provide competencies that advance careers. Examples include long-standing organizations, such as the National Association of Environmental Managers (NAEM) and National Association of Environmental Practitioners (NAEP), and more recent ones, such as the International Society of Sustainability Professionals (ISSP), Association of Climate Change Officers (ACCO), American Society of Adaptation Professionals (ASAP), and Urban Sustainability Directors Network (USDN), among many others.

This chapter emphasizes businesses and cities because they make up the majority of the world's largest and most powerful economic entities. Most people live in cities, most wealth is accumulated in cities, and most businesses service and connect cities through global supply chains. Businesses and cities, moreover, are powerful incubators of solutions to Anthropocene challenges. They also employ many sustainability professionals. Cities and the businesses that serve them have the motivation, expertise, and resources to fundamentally transform how society meets its material needs and sustains development in the Anthropocene.

Of course, people employed in public agencies and nongovernmental, social benefit organizations have critical roles to play as well, often influencing and supporting the planning and implementation activities of businesses and cities. Some of the most exciting and influential work of the Anthropocene is occurring in cross-sector spaces, where people and organizations in government, business, and social benefit sectors come together and engage in multistakeholder initiatives. Increasingly, the wicked situations of the Anthropocene require these types of multistakeholder, cross-sector engagements to address concerns that are not the domain or responsibility of any one organization or sector of society.

We begin this chapter by looking at transformations in businesses and markets, then we differentiate between government and governance and examine innovations in governance. We conclude by focusing on cities. Our purpose is to help you identify opportunities for professional advancement, career success, and influence.

Businesses and Markets

Business profitability, access to capital, market share, and competitive position increasingly respond to the sustainability challenges of the Anthropocene. Therefore, businesses integrate sustainability concerns into core corporate strategies, including operational efficiency, capital acquisition, strategic direction, and market growth. Sustainability-driven market changes could be worth 10 to 20 trillion dollars over the next few decades and much more after that.[2] Companies taking the lead in this transformation will not only dominate markets, they will determine the future of humanity. This section unpacks several of the emerging transformations:

- Sustainable purchasing
- Green capital and investment
- Employee recruitment and retention
- Corporate social responsibility
- Supply chain risks and costs
- Circular economy

Sustainable Purchasing

Many consumers prefer green, sustainable products if those products are similar to traditional products in price and quality. Some businesses are responding. For example, over the last several decades, Whirlpool intentionally improved appliance energy efficiency because it watched consumer priorities for energy efficiency move from twelfth place in the 1980s to third place today, just behind cost and performance.[3]

Strong consumer demand for sustainably produced products could, in theory, motivate businesses to transform their supply chains. However, not all customers act on their green preferences, and fewer pay extra to subsidize the added costs of producing something more sustainably (perhaps with the exceptions of green energy, organic food, and fair-trade coffee, which are rare examples of products that attract a price premium for sustainability-related attributes). Also, consumers tend to be fickle and ill-informed, and they often don't have the time to differentiate among the sustainability impacts of competing products and services. As a result, the impact of green consumer demand remains interesting but peripheral to most business operations and sustainability strategies.[4]

A few consumers in wealthier nations are intentionally buying fewer material possessions and instead buying services or digital possessions that have significantly fewer environmental impacts. This fledgling social movement goes by many names, such as "peak stuff" and "slow food." For example, the new car in the driveway matters less than the vacation destination, and the exercise bike in the basement is replaced by the fitness trainer at the gym. Status drives these consumer preferences, as it does many consumer choices. This trend of living simply with less stuff, if it accelerates, may be a consequential driver of market reform. Millennial and postmillennial generations appear to be privileging accumulation of experiences over the accumulation of stuff. We may stand on the cusp of a generational shift in consumption habits. As of now, however, it does little to motivate market transformation.

Purchasing agents and institutional buyers, in contrast, are already big drivers of market reform. They buy large quantities of products for school systems, government agencies, hotel chains, and other large organizations. These professionals possess the time and talent to evaluate products, and they increasingly demand certification that the products they purchase are produced in ways that address sustainability concerns. One of their major professional associations, the Sustainable Purchasing Leadership Council, offers training, rankings, and criteria to help members evaluate sustainable products and services. See the discussion of accountability in chapter 5 for a review of mechanisms that provide information green buyers need, including certification, labels, roundtables, and industry standards.

Green Capital and Investment

Successful businesses must acquire capital. This capital increasingly comes with green strings attached. Investors providing capital are assessing sustainability factors before making investments. The Forum for Sustainable and Responsible Investment reports that approximately one out of every three dollars under professional management in the United States is evaluated using criteria such as sustainability that identify socially responsible investments. Some of the world's largest investment companies, such as LGIM, Vital Capital Fund, Triodos Investment Management, The Reinvestment Fund, and BlueOrchard Finance S.A., now evaluate climate change and sustainability risks of the investments they recommend. If businesses want access to this green capital, they need to demonstrate that they deserve it. Morgan Stanley reports, for example, that interest in sustainable investments is at an all-time high, and people are putting their money where their mouth is: about half of the general population and two-thirds of millennials are taking part in at least one sustainable investing activity, such as investing in companies or funds that target specific environmental or social outcomes.[5]

Michael Bloomberg, founder of Bloomberg L.P. and former mayor of New York City, argues that traditional business reporting metrics are no longer sufficient. Investors now need to assess sustainability-related risks, such as supply chain vulnerabilities to water disruption, and emerging opportunities, such as new markets among the global middle class. The companies performing well on sustainability metrics also tend to perform well on financial metrics, including return on equity, cash flow stability, and dividend growth.[6]

Examples of how green strings are being attached to capital include the following:

- The Sustainable Accounting Standards Board (SASB) is "dedicated to enhancing the efficiency of the capital markets by fostering high-quality disclosure of material sustainability information that meets investor needs. . . . The SASB's transparent, inclusive, and rigorous standards-setting process is materiality focused, evidence-based and market informed." We present a full case study of SASB in chapter 13.

- The Dow Jones Sustainability™ Index requires companies to complete and share an in-depth analysis of economic, environmental, and social factors related to sustainability. Firms that lead their industries based on this assessment are listed in the high-profile index used by investors.

- CDP (formerly the Climate Disclosure Project) helps businesses understand their risks and vulnerabilities to sustainability challenges, such as climate change, greenhouse gas emissions, water usage, and deforestation. CDP reports that the number of institutional investors requesting information about these sustainable risks has increased more than twentyfold in the last ten years.

- Ceres, a nonprofit that began in 1989, largely in response to the Exxon Valdez oil spill, helps investors and stockholders assess sustainability issues and risks. They have developed numerous tools to weave environmental and social challenges into company and investor decision making, influencing hundreds of companies and trillions of dollars worth of investment.

- Principles for Responsible Investment (PRI) helps an international network of investors incorporate sustainability factors into their investment and ownership decisions, addressing everything from climate change to palm oil–driven deforestation. PRI signatories influence nearly $90 trillion of investments.
- International Finance Corporation, part of the World Bank Group, assesses its loans using environmental and social performance standards that include labor practices, resource efficiency, pollution, biodiversity, community health, involuntary resettlement, and heritage resources. Importantly, these standards are rippling through all public and private financial institutions wanting to do business with the World Bank institutions and hence changing finance practices around the globe.

Employee Recruitment and Retention

A company's sustainability profile impacts employee recruitment and retention. Most organizations report difficulties retaining staff. Surveys show that one in four new hires will leave within six months and 50 percent leave within two years. Turnover can cost multiple times an employee's salary because of severance pay, lost productivity, lost opportunities, and expensive recruitment and training processes.[7]

Millennials will make up 75 percent of the workforce in 2025. More than 70 percent of millennials want their employers to focus on societal or mission-driven issues, such as sustainability. But regardless of their generation, most employees increase productivity and retention when their companies and their work have clear social relevance, such as sustainable development. Thus companies with a clear and effective sustainability ethos are not just better at attracting and retaining employees, they are also more productive.[8]

Corporate Social Responsibility

Corporations are, by definition and by law, publicly sanctioned entities with obligations to serve the interests of both the public and shareholders. Addressing local and global sustainability issues is increasingly expected as part of a corporation's social license to operate.[9]

Corporate philanthropy often targets sustainability issues such as poverty reduction, clean water, economic development, and human rights. Take The Coca-Cola Company as a well-studied example. They focus their considerable philanthropic and strategic resources on—among other things—water, women, and community well-being. Coca-Cola is convinced that women entrepreneurs have immediate and lasting impacts on their communities. Most of their Ekocenters kiosks, for example, are managed by women. These kiosks provide clean water, internet connectivity, solar-powered electricity, jobs, and, of course, Coca-Cola products in some of the most remote and distressed regions of the world.

The UN Global Compact illustrates progressive efforts by many business leaders to envision a sustainable and inclusive global economy that delivers lasting benefits to people, communities, and markets, while protecting key environmental qualities. Approximately 9,000 companies have pledged to abide by and report progress on the Global Compact's ten principles, which focus on human rights, labor, environment, and corruption. Many large global businesses also embrace the UN Sustainable Development Goals (SDGs). Stalwarts of energy-intensive global capitalism, such as Occidental Petroleum and Toyota, have made bold claims to go carbon neutral. The CEO of Cargill, one of the world's largest aggregators and traders of agricultural commodities, publicly warns about the need to address climate change. In addition, business-facing trade organizations, such as the Business Roundtable and the World Business Council for Sustainable Development, explicitly focus on businesses' obligations to shape and respond to challenges of the Anthropocene.

Cost and Risk Management

Businesses have minimized waste since the beginning of capitalism, long before the term "sustainable development" was coined. Profits increase with more efficient (and less) use of material and energy inputs, as well as with declining costs of waste processing and disposal. The Anthropocene presents a new set of risks and costs for businesses to minimize.[10]

Climate change, the poster child of the Anthropocene, gets factored into basic business calculations and operations because, to point out just a few reasons, floods and storms disrupt transportation, frost and drought disrupt agricultural production, heat waves threaten worker health and safety, and wildfires disrupt everything.[11] Insurance companies, as a specific example, adjust rates and coverage for flood and hurricane damage. Likewise, utilities that provide water, power, and sanitation now strategically invest in becoming more redundant and thus less vulnerable to weather extremes. Disruptions caused by the COVID-19 pandemic, for example, drove home the need to build redundancies into supply chains previously designed for just-in-time efficiency. Traditional business consultancies, such as Pricewaterhouse-Coopers, McKinsey, and Ernst and Young, now offer services helping businesses manage risks from climate change and other disruptions becoming more likely in the Anthropocene.

Take water as an example of another Anthropocene challenge. Iconic water-intensive companies, such as Coca-Cola and Anheuser-Busch InBev, have impressive water management strategies to reduce water-related risks. They are driving down water use within the walls of their factories, so much so that producing a liter of product now uses only slightly more than one liter of water. They also monitor and manage their source water vulnerabilities because most of the water on which their businesses depend is used outside factory walls; for example, in irrigating the grains and sugars that go into soda and beer. Water issues also create huge reputational risks because water is so intimately connected to residential and community well-being. For example, concerns about the misuse of a community's water in Kerala, India, forced Coca-Cola to close a plant and pay tens of millions of dollars for perceived damage to the community's groundwater.[12] Aqueduct, a web-accessible platform built by Coca-Cola but expanded and maintained by the World Resources Institute, helps businesses assess their exposure to water-related risks.

Circular Economy

The holy grail of sustainable development is decoupling economic growth from environmental impact. The effort goes by several names, including decoupling, dematerializing, cradle-to-cradle, ecological modernization, regeneration, and circular economy. The topic was mentioned in chapter 2 because a circular economy is a solution to the linear economy's take–make–waste-disposal of finite resources, which presents a significant bottleneck to sustaining development in an increasingly wealthy and materialistic world.

A circular economy goes well beyond recycling, because recycling is often down-cycling as materials get diluted, compromised, and less usable. A truly circular economy keeps finite materials in use rather than in dumps. Achieving it will require new technologies and production systems. Durable goods such as cars and refrigerators need to be designed for disassembly and reuse. Goods subject to rapid technological advance, such as phones, need to be designed for upgrading rather than replacing. Consumers must change their mindset: we must rent or share rather than own. Businesses must also change their mindset: they must sell services rather than sell goods.

Businesses are motivated to construct a circular economy because it gives them more control over inputs, reducing the risks and uncertainty of finding, harvesting, processing, and transporting materials.[13] Malthusian arguments about finite resources become irrelevant because materials will be continuously reused.

The total financial implications are huge. Resource demand is on pace to double over the next decade. Without changing the linear, cradle-to-disposal business model, predictions suggest an eight billion ton shortfall of natural resources by 2030—approximately equivalent to everything used by North American economies in 2014. The resulting price hikes, supply variability, and risks associated with this shortfall translate to $4.5 trillion of lost economic growth by 2030 and as much as $25 trillion by 2050. The UN International Resource Panel estimates that wisely circulating rather than discarding materials can not only offset the cost of mitigating climate change, it can also add several trillion dollars to the global economy. E-waste, for example, is the fastest-growing waste stream in the world: we annually discard fifty million metric tons of phones, TVs, computers, and other electronics, weighing more than all of the commercial airliners ever made. This waste is worth over $60 billion: there is 100 times more gold in a metric ton of smartphones than in a typical metric ton of gold ore. Currently, only 20 percent of e-waste gets reused.[14]

Consider Ricoh, a global consumer products company. It recently concluded that, by 2050, supply disruptions of virgin materials used in manufacturing its office equipment, cameras, and other products will disrupt its business operations. It therefore used circular economy thinking to plan how to reduce, by 87.5 percent, the use of virgin resources it expects by 2050. It plans to do so by improving resource utilization and by improved recovery and recycling of products and materials.[15]

Businesses are also motivated to construct a circular economy because it creates new opportunities to add value, and hence to increase market share and profit. The circular economy creates a new and more intimate relationship between businesses and consumers, not ending at the point-of-sale but continuing through use, maintenance, and resale or return. Companies will need to adopt a service-dominant logic rather than a product-dominant logic. Some products will be rented rather than sold, and returned to the manufacturer after use or when in need of upgrading. For example, Lauren Phipps of GreenBiz writes that a growing number of clothing brands provide customers the option to rent rather than buy outfits. The economics and logistics are still being sorted out, and they might work best for high-end, special-event products like wedding dresses and camping gear; but it is indicative of a high-impact industry—fashion—responding to changing market challenges. Businesses can also use their marketing prowess: for a fee, they can connect the original buyer, who no longer needs the product, with new customers who can use it, thereby facilitating reuse. Similarly, business marketing and logistic skills can support the emerging "sharing economy." Many products often sit idle, such as cars. In developed economies, up to 80 percent of things stored in a typical home get used only once a month. Maintaining shared products and managing the sharing platforms create enormous new business opportunities (think Airbnb or Uber).[16]

Perhaps the most challenging transition required by the circular economy will be getting consumers to accept new forms of ownership, product design, and use agreements. The circular economy reimagines the consumer as someone who uses a service rather than consumes a product. The contract between businesses and their customers becomes based on continued performance rather than final sale. Consumers need to accept renting rather than owning, trading with other users, sharing payment and use for goods not in their sole possession, upgrades and buy-back options rather than disposing of the old and buying the new, and purchasing service agreements instead of products. A fully circular economy is still a long way off, but examples abound, and there are more on the horizon.

Cross-Sector Governance

Here at the dawn of the Anthropocene, humans are changing the environment in novel ways and at scales that threaten human health and economic development globally. Market transformations, such as those already discussed, are necessary, but likely to be insufficient for steering our accelerating development trajectory through the narrowing bottleneck of wicked challenges; we also need transformations in governance. Throughout history, whenever and wherever humans degraded environmental conditions enough to threaten their own health and economy, the societies with better governance achieved greater prosperity and longer lives.[17] Laissez-faire environmental governance, which places minimal limits on individual and market freedoms, suffices only when humans are few and their environmental impacts do not harm other people.

Understanding new models of governance emerging in response to Anthropocene challenges is key to understanding how you can exercise influence, how you will be influenced, and how you can advance your career. Importantly, governance can occur without government. Once we accept the possibility of governance without government, countless opportunities emerge to influence sustainable development, including many of the wicked leadership practices discussed later in this book.

"Government" is a territorially limited set of organizations sanctioned and specialized to manage collective matters (i.e., health and safety) at various levels of social organization (i.e., nation, state, city). Modern nations, for example, are a combination of territory, authority, and rights; a model that emerged out of the 1648 Treaty of Westphalia. Before then, these government entities that we now take for granted did not exist;

instead, there were overlapping territorial claims by local princes, the church, cities, and regional lords.[18] In the US, states, counties, and cities are examples of territorial organizations with governmental authority.

"Governance" is the set of social functions and processes that people use to guide behaviors and decisions. Governments practice governance, but governance is broader and not limited to what governments do. Most governance is informal, such as norms, traditions, and expectations that guide behavior. Alliances, associations, roundtables, and coalitions all depend on governance policies that guide behavior and expectations. Sometimes the governance structure is formal, such as in partnerships and contracts.

Cross-sector governance strategies are necessary because the wicked challenges of the Anthropocene exceed the capacities of any one organization and any one sector. As a result, some of the most interesting innovations for sustainability are occurring in the cross-sector space where government, business, and nongovernmental organizations (NGOs) overlap. These governance strategies use differences as an asset—differences in resources, experience, demographics, and perspective—to take on wicked challenges.[19]

Cross-sector governance arrangements are now so common in sustainability practice that it is hard to imagine a time when it was not so. But as recently as 1992, the United Nations Conference on Environment and Development found it needed to formally state that government actions, alone, were proving insufficient and to call for better cross-sector governance models to help government, business, and civil society collaborate. As a result, NGOs began retooling and broadening their focus, from mostly trying to influence government actors to also trying to directly influence market actors, a practice that is now widespread and seems normal.

The shift toward cross-sector governance accelerated with the 2002 World Summit on Sustainable Development, which further promoted cross-sector collaboration using names such as "hybrid governance" and "type II" partnerships. The then UN secretary general, Kofi Annan, predicted that cross-sector collaboration would become the most important and powerful agent of change. Neoliberal policies deepened this trend by promoting privatization, outsourcing government services, and otherwise assigning to market actors responsibilities previously exercised only by governments.[20]

In addition to bringing different resources and talents to the table, cross-sector governance strategies can lower costs, be more nimble, and produce less social friction than government-enforced regulations. These attributes are needed if we are to address the vast, dynamic, and politically charged challenges and opportunities of the Anthropocene. Moreover, cross-sector governance strategies can work across political and trade boundaries, and persist beyond election cycles and quarterly investment reports. Further, many cross-sector governance structures are global, hence accelerating innovation by sharing understandings of sustainability challenges and innovative solutions worldwide. Several examples of cross-sector governance serve to illustrate its utility and flexibility for tackling wicked challenges of the Anthropocene (Figure 3.1).

- Governments can collaborate with community groups to co-manage publicly owned forests and fisheries in efforts known as community-based natural resource management. In these efforts, desired goals are jointly agreed upon, and the resources therefore are jointly managed. The government (national, provincial, or local) does not abdicate its legal management responsibilities for the resources; rather, the planning and uses of the resources are developed in tandem with stakeholders, who lack direct management authority but who have close proximity and high interest.
- Governments can collaborate with businesses by forming public–private partnerships to outsource routine public functions, such as

school lunches, prison operations, concessions, and mineral leases. In some cases, the role of government clearly overlaps with the private sector capacity, and the private sector may be better suited to deliver such goods and services. In other cases, such as schools and prisons, outsourcing remains contested.

- Businesses can collaborate with NGOs and government agencies using "roundtables" to develop industry standards, third-party certifications, and product labels that set and monitor supply chain operations and impacts.[21]
- Businesses, community groups, NGOs, and government actors collaborate to manage and pay for ecosystem services that government regulation or market forces working alone can no longer guarantee. As an example, forest-to-faucet programs collect fees from downstream water consumers to pay upstream landowners to maintain forest land cover that filters and stores water.

Cross-sector governance is by no means a panacea.[22] By their design, these arrangements are self-monitored by collaborators and thus can be less transparent and accountable to the broader public than government programs. Power and influence become concentrated in the collaborators, who understandably act in their own self-interests, which may not be representative of the public at large. Unfortunately, little is known about the durability of these efforts. Because these governance arrangements are voluntary, participation and funding can wane and cease. The use of voluntary approaches may be more problematic for sustainability challenges requiring high rates of participation and compliance across diverse actors, such as carbon tax or cap-and-trade on greenhouse gas emissions. They also may struggle when accountability is poor, free ridership is high, enforcement is difficult, and only the best actors in the sector volunteer to participate. Finally, cross-sector governance solutions sometimes privatize aspects of the environment that provide basic

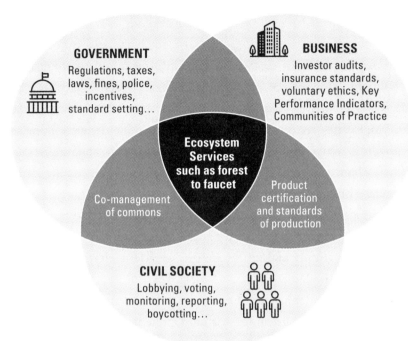

Figure 3.1. Example of sustainability governance tools by sector and across sectors. Opportunities for governance extend well beyond what government can do. (Adapted from Magali A. Delmas and Oran R. Young, eds. *Governance for the Environment: New Perspectives* [Cambridge, UK: Cambridge University Press, 2009].)

human rights, such as clean air, water, and the ecosystem services that support life. Privatization necessarily limits access, thus raising concerns about equity and social justice.

The emergence of these new governance models does not diminish the essential role for good governments. Sustainable development requires stable, competent government operations able to establish and enforce laws, minimize corruption, promote public interests, and incentivize desirable behaviors and norms. Ensuring stable property rights and the rule of law, and holding a monopoly on violence are uniquely suited to government. Some of the most effective government units today are cities.

Cities

Cities may be the most motivated, most informed, and most engaged government actors of the early Anthropocene.[23] Their ability to provide basic services to citizens is already threatened by Anthropocene conditions. They are on the receiving end of specific, tangible impacts of flooding, water pollution, food scarcity, wildfires, and migration. Climate change, for example, is requiring major investments in infrastructure—bridges, water treatment plants, energy utilities, and health care facilities need to be upgraded or replaced. Insurance costs are skyrocketing. Economic and climate refugees migrating to urban areas in search of opportunity and refuge are overwhelming city infrastructure and public safety.

Cities are a fundamentally different type of government institution than the nations they are nested within. Unlike many national governments, cities simply do not have the luxury of deferring decisions or actions. Mayors and city officials are held accountable, and hence they are acting, forming alliances, and innovating solutions.[24] For example, in chapter 11, we present a case study of a municipality near Washington, DC, that figured out how to decrease its greenhouse gas emissions and become carbon-neutral by 2050. Critically, cities have the wealth, talent, and political will to respond to challenges of the Anthropocene.

This is good news because cities are critical to sustainable development. Cities are responsible for two-thirds of the world's energy consumption and perhaps 80 percent of economic production, and they directly or indirectly generate 70 percent of global greenhouse gas emissions. Cities are one of our most effective engines for pulling people and nations out of poverty. Throughout human history cities have been centers of human rights, creativity, health care, and culture. Cities, critically, facilitate exchange of goods, services, ideas, and technologies. Cities are where differences mix and mingle, producing innovations and inventions.

Importantly, urbanism, as a rule, reduces per person environmental impacts.[25] Good urbanism concentrates people in higher density, leaving land for habitat and ecosystem services.[26] Urbanites, per person and on average, commute less, consume less energy, and live in smaller homes than their rural and suburban counterparts of comparable wealth. Residents of New York City, for example, own fewer vehicles and use far less energy commuting than the average American. The average US rural household consumes 27 percent more electricity than an urban household, in part because typical rural, single-family homes are detached and don't share common walls. And, of course, urban households tend to be stacked vertically, saving land, water, and chemicals needed to beautify lawns. Smart growth, green infrastructure, green building, and related approaches to good urbanization provide some of the most powerful levers for sustainable development.

Cities are connected virtually and globally, embedded in a web that creates both redundancies and vulnerabilities. Finances, supply chains, energy, talent—it all moves to and from cities around the globe. Cities must manage these flows if they are to sustain development. All cities face similar pragmatic concerns, creating an environment of cooperation, unlike the self-serving and seemingly inescapable competition among nation-states. Cities are becoming the most innovative and powerful institutions capable of illuminating governance paths forward at a global scale.

As an example, take the city of Dubai in the United Arab Emirates, which has a goal of becoming one of the most sustainable cities on Earth.[27] Dubai has grown from a sleepy pearl-diving community to one of the most striking urban settings to be found anywhere in the world. It is home to the world's tallest skyscraper and the world's most expensive hotel, an indoor ski slope set in a desert, and one of the highest per-capita water uses in the world. Due to its location on the edge of the desert and its dearth of natural resources, Dubai's foodstuffs are imported, its water is desalinated, much of its high-value real estate is being built at sea level on man-made islands, and 85 percent of its workforce constantly flows in and out of the city. Dubai is also one of the world's largest air travel hubs, and it is home to a critical cargo port connecting Europe and Asia. No matter how you slice it, Dubai is a prime example of how highly connected modern cities are, how highly reliant they are on the integrity and resilience of those connections, and how important sustainability and trends of the Anthropocene are. To mitigate what are essentially existential risks, cities such as Dubai are increasingly acting preemptively to address water, food, energy, and climate challenges; often despite national lethargy.

Cities learn from one another and lead change beyond their borders by working with other cities, businesses, and other public and private partners. For example, highly influential city-led learning and action networks include long-standing organizations, such as United Cities and Local Governments (UCLG) and Local Governments for Sustainability (aka ICLEI), and more recent and emergent entities, such as the Urban Sustainability Directors Network (USDN), C40 Cities Climate Leadership Group, Carbon Neutral Cities Alliance, and the Alliance for a Sustainable Future. All of these organizations connect business and cities in joint efforts for sustainable development.

Conclusion

Careers and employment opportunities addressing sustainability issues are increasingly common, respected, and well compensated. This chapter has examined transformations of markets, governance, and cities: the major institutions of our world that provide you with opportunities for career advancement and influence over sustainable development.

Clearly, markets are transforming. This is good news because sustainable development requires getting the market right, which means businesses-as-usual must change. Will the transformations happen fast enough, before industrial capitalism consumes its foundation and collapses? That question should keep us up at night. Market failures continue to worsen the bottleneck challenges to sustainable development reviewed in the previous chapter. Not all of these market failures can be corrected by voluntary efforts guided by the enlightened self-interest of profit-driven business actors. Needed change will be delayed by stubborn, entrenched, institutionalized pressures, such as short-termism, limited liability, corruption, iron triangles, and corporations' unfettered access to influence political campaigns.

New partnerships, new institutions, new forms of governance, and new roles for governments will be required. Fortunately, new forms of governance are also emerging. Society's sustainable development depends on these ongoing transformations of markets and governance, and on leadership and innovation by cross-sector initiatives. Your career and influence depend on your ability to see and engage these transformations. The next chapter begins a deep dive into leadership tools you will need in order to have influence in the world that these transformations are creating.

PART II

Toolbox for Wicked Leadership

CHAPTER 4

Leadership Basics

Climate change, water scarcity, poverty, linear economy, and other Anthropocene challenges are "wicked" situations that require people to connect, collaborate, and adapt. These challenges require coordinating the goals, actions, and commitments of countless, differentially motivated, widely distributed actors working in different organizations and responsible to different authorities. Wicked problems require navigating controversial topics that polarize and divide people. They require comprehending and influencing situations that are emergent, dynamic, erratic, uncertain, novel, and teleconnected. They require systems thinking to tackle root causes embedded in multiscalar, complex, and evolving situations. They require everyone—you included—to lead from where you are. This chapter introduces leadership practices for these wicked situations.

Leadership Defined

It boils down to three concepts: direction, alignment, and commitment.[1] Leadership occurs when stakeholders agree on a direction for their efforts, align their resources as needed to achieve that direction, and commit to delivering those resources as well as supporting each other. Stated differently, things get done when stakeholders achieve direction, alignment, and commitment. Actions happen: goals are attempted, resources deployed, strategies engaged. Anywhere and anytime leadership occurs, you will find direction, alignment, and commitment. The recipe is simple in principle but difficult in practice. When it works, the results can be life-changing, as described in the story "Leadership Is a Key Ingredient in Water" (chapter 10).

All three conditions—direction, alignment, and commitment—must be present for leadership to occur (Figure 4.1). You are probably familiar with frustrating situations in which one or more of these conditions has been absent. For example, when stakeholders have direction but no alignment, they agree on a mission statement, but, perhaps because they are competitors for funding, will not share resources or will neglect to complete important but unrewarding tasks. Conversely, if stakeholders have commitment but lack direction or alignment, people head off in all directions at once, often working at cross-purposes as well as risking burnout and damaging the reputation of the group. Most perversely, a group can have direction and alignment but no commitment, so time, money, and goodwill get wasted; or, worse, the effort gets sabotaged.

Who is responsible for facilitating direction, alignment, and commitment (i.e., who practices leadership)? In wicked situations, the answer is EVERYONE. In fact, direction, alignment, and commitment cannot be achieved in wicked situations without shared participation by many stakeholders. That means you should practice leadership regardless of your position or status in the hierarchy. As we explain in this chapter, traditional conceptions of leadership—a single leader inspiring followers to follow—won't work well in wicked situations. These traditional models of leadership are designed for nonwicked situations and emphasize attributes and actions of leaders that motivate followers.[2] For

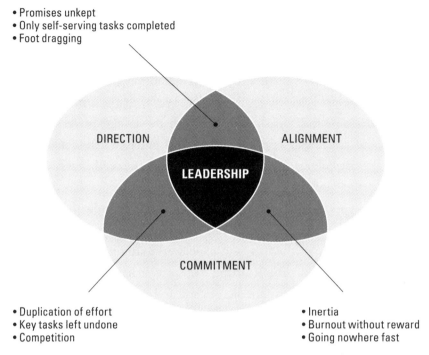

- Promises unkept
- Only self-serving tasks completed
- Foot dragging

DIRECTION   ALIGNMENT

LEADERSHIP

COMMITMENT

- Duplication of effort
- Key tasks left undone
- Competition

- Inertia
- Burnout without reward
- Going nowhere fast

Figure 4.1. Leadership described. These three conditions are present whenever and wherever leadership helps a group get things done. (Adapted from the Center for Creative Leadership.)

example, leaders are supposed to be authentic, bold, charismatic, honest, empathetic, visionary, and good communicators and storytellers. You are no doubt familiar with popularized accounts emphasizing the acts and attributes of individual leaders: Margaret Thatcher, Abraham Lincoln, Mahatma Gandhi, or Steve Jobs. These narratives focus on "great" people and their leadership characteristics. This leader–follower approach to leadership is sufficient for many conditions but, we argue here, it is insufficient for wicked situations in which leadership responsibility must be distributed and shared.

Leadership guru Ronald Heifetz, in *Leadership without Easy Answers*, offers a thought experiment to illustrate a critical difference between the shared–distributed approach to leadership and the leader–follower approach. He asks us to compare the responsibilities, processes, and outcomes that result from the two approaches. In the leader–follower approach, a vision of the desired future condition and the process for getting there are selected by the leader, and if that vision or process is inaccurate or misguided, fault lies with the leader. In the shared–distributed leadership approach, direction emerges from the stakeholders. Stakeholders must hold themselves accountable both for the processes they use to create that future and for the future they create; if something goes wrong, the responsibility collectively lies with the stakeholders. The different approaches to leadership inspire different roles, processes, and responsibilities, and likely lead to different outcomes.

For the wicked situations of the Anthropocene, such as those outlined in chapter 2, direction, alignment, and commitment cannot be imposed from above—no one has authority over the widely diverse and distributed stakeholders (Box 4.1). Moreover, as we will unpack here, no one person, and often no one organization or sector of society, can know in advance how to solve or even how to define wicked situations. In wicked situations, stakeholders must simultaneously co-construct both the "problem" and the "solution." Stakeholders must work—peer-to-peer—to learn what the challenges and opportunities are, to decide what values they will enhance or compromise, to negotiate which futures are acceptable and unacceptable, to assess what strategies will safely create the desired future conditions, and to commit to repeated failure and revision as they learn by doing to create that future.

Nothing in this conception of leadership diminishes the critical roles played by people in recognized leadership positions: those at the top of the hierarchy, elected or promoted to corner offices, with authority over people and budgets in their organizations and networks. In many situations, direction, alignment, and/or commitment can't be achieved without them. But, still, for reasons reviewed above and illustrated through

Box 4.1. Unpacking Direction, Alignment, and Commitment

Direction

To paraphrase Yogi Berra, if you don't know where you are going, you'll end up someplace else. Strong direction exists when stakeholders agree on what they are aiming to accomplish, what success looks like, and how they are going to accomplish their shared goals. Ronald Heifetz, in *Leadership without Easy Answers*, calls the work of constructing direction "adaptive work," which he defines as the process of learning and articulating the gap between aspirations and reality. Getting direction is rarely easy. It may involve orchestrating conflict and exposing internal contradictions that mobilize people to clarify what matters most and what can be traded off. In wicked situations, when conditions are changing and clouded by uncertainty, such clarity is difficult to achieve and requires a process of continuously creating and refining direction.

Solutions to sustainability challenges, such as climate change, urbanization, and poverty, always produce both winners and losers. Fortunes, identities, and lifestyles are at stake, so people care deeply about the direction chosen and the outcomes produced. Agreeing on direction often requires identifying, exposing, and managing the resulting conflicts. Many stakeholders, when they first assess a wicked situation and begin a collaborative process, only vaguely understand their own goals. The situation is novel and the future uncertain. Their goals get shaped and refined by testing their hopes and dreams against reality, by comparing their own hopes and dreams to those of others, and by measuring their goals against what is practical and possible. Only through hard work, openness, and honesty can a shared vision of the future be constructed and agreed to. Importantly, the agreed-upon direction will likely change and be retargeted as stakeholders learn from, and with, each other, and from encountering the future they co-create. Without direction, would-be collaborators are uncertain about what they should accomplish together and may feel pulled in different directions by competing goals.

Alignment

Stakeholders must coordinate their efforts to do the work needed to produce the desired outcomes. Stakeholders achieve alignment when their time, talent, and resources are coordinated so that all necessary activities occur at the

continued on next page

right times and places. Diverse stakeholders bring different resources to bear: they have different expertise, pull different levers, and exercise different types of influence. Some tasks are glamorous and thus generate too many volunteers. Other tasks are less popular because they are expensive, risky, boring, or thankless.

Alignment is particularly challenging in large systems typical of sustainability challenges, such as a watershed, a city, or a supply chain, because stakeholders are so widely distributed that they don't normally interact and may not be aware of each other. Alignment can also be difficult when actors have long-lasting and complicated relationships. Would-be partners that need to align their efforts might have a history of competing for the same funding, market segment, or constituency, and thus fear collaboration because it could be interpreted as losing out to or being co-opted by the competition. As is the case with direction, alignment needs to be flexible and responsive to the changing context. Stakeholders with weak alignment work in isolation and don't see how their tasks fit into the larger set of tasks to be done. They risk working at cross-purposes, duplicating effort, or having important work fall through the cracks.

Commitment

Even if stakeholders agree in which direction to aim and on what resources to align to make that happen, the effort will still falter unless everyone is committed. Actors must willingly sacrifice some self-interests and be willing to invest their own resources to achieve shared goals. Stakeholders with strong commitment feel responsible for the success and well-being of the collective effort, and they know that other stakeholders feel the same. They trust one another, will stick with the effort through difficult times, and will allow other stakeholders to make demands on their time and energy.

Levels of commitment will vary between stakeholders and may wax and wane over time. Like direction and alignment, commitment must be actively managed through an iterative process of monitoring, evaluation, and revision. Stakeholders with weak commitment put their own interests ahead of others and contribute only when it is easy or in their self-interest to do so. If commitment does not exist, then people make promises but don't follow through—or worse, drag their feet and sabotage progress. Apathy, risk aversion, and "what can I do" shrugs are frustratingly common responses that indicate lack of commitment.

the remainder of this book, these few individuals can't do it alone. Navigating the challenges of the Anthropocene requires both strong leadership from above as well as shared leadership from below, the middle, outside-in, and inside-out.

Hopefully you find this conception of leadership empowering. All of us can, and should, lead from where we are—you included. All of us, regardless of our position, can help promote direction, alignment, and commitment. All of us can, and should, practice leadership, especially in wicked situations such as those we face in the Anthropocene.

Leadership Practices for Wicked Problems

The direction–alignment–commitment theory of leadership has enormous power and generalizability. It works in most cultures, contexts, and situations. However—and this is important—the practices that produce direction, alignment, and commitment vary by situation. This section introduces three sets of leadership practices appropriate for wicked situations: practices that help *connect* across space and time, *collaborate* across differences, and *adapt* to uncertainty (Figure 4.2). While these leadership practices are especially useful in wicked situations, such as the social and environmental Anthropocene challenges discussed in chapter 2, many of the practices also work in both tame and crisis situations.

Connect

Wicked situations have connections that span space, time, and cultures. Stakeholders, causes, effects, resources, risks, and other key factors are distributed across vast, complicated, global systems, such as watersheds, food systems, supply chains, and, in the case of climate change, the entire biosphere. Factors that must be influenced are so widely dispersed across political, economic, and organizational boundaries that they are hard to connect and influence in any coordinated fashion. Conventional,

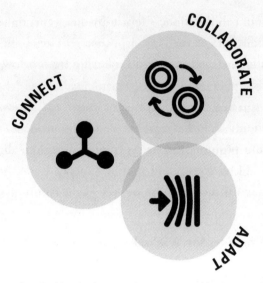

Figure 4.2. Types of wicked leadership practices presented in chapters 5, 6, and 7.

hierarchical leadership often does not, or cannot, appreciate the degree of connectedness of Anthropocene challenges because of institutional incentives, boundaries, and blinders that limit the scope of a leader's vision and imagination.

Alarmingly, risks and impacts that were previously isolated can, because of the scale and pace of anthropogenically driven change, connect and aggregate to create tipping points for dangerous system-wide change. Conversely, isolated solutions, no matter how innovative and effective, will produce drop-in-the-bucket impacts that are insufficient to affect the large-scale, system-wide changes that are needed (i.e., solutions must be scaled and coordinated).

Moreover, no one has authority over all the stakeholders who must be engaged because stakeholders are distributed across different organizations, nations, and professions. Most actors will neither meet nor interact, and some may not even realize they are connected; yet their actions must be coordinated if the needed system-wide change is to occur. Without coordination, the actions of some stakeholders can negate the actions of others, as in the case of long supply chains where sustainability impacts accumulate through resource extraction, industrial production, packaging, transport, storage, sale, purchase, use, and disposal. In situations such as climate change and supply chains, the challenge is especially complicated because the people trying to solve the problem are connected to, or in some cases the very same, people causing the problem.

Chapter 5 explains wicked leadership practices promoting connections across space and time. They are summarized in Table 4.1.

Collaborate

Wicked situations exceed the capacities of any one organization, and even any one sector (e.g., market, government, or civil society). Solutions require stakeholders to collaborate despite vast differences in their values, assumptions, personalities, disciplines, professions, generations, cultures, and sectors. Most stakeholders are trapped in silos of similarity that are self-reinforcing and protectionist, accentuating differences that hinder efforts to collaborate across those silos. Collaboration is further complicated because the wicked challenges of the Anthropocene are exceptionally ambiguous and ill-defined. Stakeholders rarely agree on what the problem is or what outcomes they want to accomplish. And even if they agree on outcomes, they likely disagree on the strategy to achieve those outcomes (e.g., should the strategy be a voluntary, market-led innovation or a government-led regulation?).

Win–win solutions may not be possible in wicked situations. Stakeholders must compromise, make difficult choices and trade-offs, or change their values and behaviors—which is a particularly heavy lift for most people and many organizations because doing so threatens relationships, challenges identity, and questions the status quo. Stakeholders must do this difficult work; it can't be done for them. They must

Table 4.1. Leadership Practices for Connecting Across Space and Time (Chapter 5)

Accountability	Being transparent about sustainability impacts holds people accountable for their actions because they take credit or avoid shame and blame.
Storytelling	Stories organize facts, explain why things happen, illustrate roles people play, and coordinate action.
Community of practice	Professionals can learn from each other and become more effective in their respective practices.
Train-the-trainer	Training creates a ripple effect of people training others who train others, connecting and spreading expertise throughout the system.
Scaling-up	Replicating isolated innovations in multiple locations can produce system change rather than insignificant, drop-in-the-bucket impacts.
Diffusion	Characteristics of innovations and networks can lead to successfully spreading the innovation throughout the network.
Collective impact	Organizing multiple, dispersed, and sometimes competing stakeholders enables their simultaneously applied efforts to have system-wide impact, exceeding by far the sum of their otherwise isolated and piecemeal efforts.
Information campaigns	Information rarely changes behavior, but carefully organized social marketing campaigns can.

voluntarily share, defend, and change their interests and positions. It must be voluntary because no stakeholder has power or authority over all other stakeholders, and because changes in value cannot be enforced or imposed if commitment is to be sustained. Wicked situations are wicked, in part, because stakeholders must do the hard work of agreeing to what needs doing, how to do it, and who wins and loses because of it.

Table 4.2. Leadership Practices for Collaborating Across Differences (Chapter 6)

Riding elephants	Characteristics of human nature include confirmation bias, identity-protective reasoning, filter bubbles, and echo chambers.
Picking battles	Not everyone will be equally receptive to your efforts to bridge differences, and some, because of network propaganda loops, may be completely inaccessible. Focus your efforts where they can best produce results.
Don't rely on facts (but when you do…)	Accept human tendency to cherry-pick facts, and agree on criteria by which facts become facts. Facilitate joint fact finding. Clarify conflict. Complicate the narrative. Use images and graphs.
Manage identity	Trigger group membership. Affirm self-worth. Play nice. Say "Yes, and…." Minimize identity conflict. Reframe the story.
Span boundaries and synergize differences	Become self-aware. Learn how to explain yourself. Respect differences. Practice active listening. Attempt empathy. Focus on interests and values, not positions and solutions.
Trust and trust repair	Some components of trust can be managed (affective, rational, and system) and lost trust can be repaired.
Partnering	Use practices that help long-term and in-depth collaborations succeed.

Chapter 6 explains wicked leadership practices promoting collaboration across differences. They are summarized in Table 4.2.

Adapt

Wicked situations require adapting to overwhelming uncertainty and change. Uncertainty is on the rise because the environmental stability of the Holocene is waning while disruptive technological and social innovation are accelerating. Moreover, increased connectivity, already discussed, further increases uncertainty because impacts ripple back and forth through the system in unpredictable ways. Dynamic and emergent situations make causation less knowable and control less possible. Problem-solving approaches that rely on analysis, prediction, and control will struggle in these conditions.

Because conditions are new and changing, solutions that worked in the past may not work in the future. New technologies and strategies will be needed, some creating novel impacts that compound uncertainty. The fickleness of stakeholders adds yet more uncertainty. Stakeholders learn and change as they encounter each other and as they encounter the new conditions created by their interventions. Their changing values and actions will be feedback loops that create new, unique system dynamics that require new interventions and course corrections, that in turn require repeated engagement, learning, and compromise.

Chapter 7 explains wicked leadership practices for adapting to the confounding change and uncertainty of wicked situations. They are summarized in Table 4.3.

Wicked Problems Unpacked

The two main points made so far in this chapter are (1) leadership happens and groups of people get things done when direction, alignment, and commitment are all present; and (2) three sets of leadership practices—connecting, collaborating, and adapting—help people get things done when situations are wicked. That's pretty much all you need to know to make sense of the rest of the book. But if you want to better understand wicked problems and why they require special leadership practices, then read this section. It examines attributes of "wicked" problems and contrasts them with "tame" and "crisis" problems (Figure 4.3). In the tables and text that follow, the attributes of tame, crisis, and wicked problems are sorted into three categories: scale, diversity, and

Table 4.3. Leadership Practices for Adapting to Uncertainty and Change (Chapter 7)

Sensemaking	Avoid analysis paralysis by mapping systems, stakeholders, strategies, and outcomes.
Learn by doing	Treat failure constructively and as an opportunity to learn, using the plan-do-test-fix approach and single, double, and triple-loop learning.
Innovation	Assemble social entrepreneurs to question the status quo, envision alternatives, and test, pivot, and scale innovations to problems mired in high uncertainty.
Be disruptive	Rock the boat and challenge the status quo if needed.
Resiliency	Adopt forward-looking, capacity-enhancing goals, such as resilience.
Scenario planning	Articulate a pathway into the future and what it would take to create it.
Sharing lessons	Engage stakeholders and inform them of changing agendas and lessons learned.

uncertainty. These categories parallel the three categories of leadership practices: connect, collaborate, and adapt.

A tame problem may be highly complex, and solving it may require advanced expertise, but the situation is familiar, something similar has been solved previously, and resources and capacities can be assembled to solve it again (Table 4.4). Example tame problems include improving the energy efficiency of mass-produced cars or constructing an energy-neutral building. The teams, organizations, and partnerships needed to manage the problem already exist. Clear lines of authority and responsibility already exist. And agreement already exists as to what constitutes a successful outcome. Outcomes can be anticipated because past experience and knowledge from science allow meaningful predictions about cause–effect relationships. The system is relatively stable,

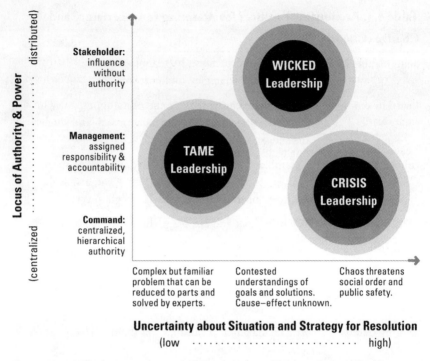

Figure 4.3. Leadership varies by situation type. (Adapted from Keith Grint, "Problems, Problems, Problems: The Social Construction of 'Leadership,'" *Human Relations* 58, no. 11 [2005]: 1467–1494.)

self-contained, and controllable, so outcomes can be disassembled, worked on independently, and reassembled. However, just because a problem is tame does not mean that leadership is easy. Many efforts to solve tame problems fail because of ineffective leadership. It can be exceedingly difficult to identify, organize, motivate, and allocate the needed people and resources.

A crisis (Table 4.5) so clearly threatens life and livelihood that stakeholders willingly set aside their differences and accept someone else's authority, at least until people feel safe, get their bearings, and chart the next steps. An example crisis would be a major hurricane that disrupts water, power, and public safety. Uncertainty is so high that stakeholders

Table 4.4. Attributes of Tame Problems

Problem definition	Scales across which stakeholders must connect	Diversity across which stakeholders must collaborate	Uncertainties to which stakeholders must adapt
• Familiar; encountered before • Agreed-upon problem to fix • Reducible to parts • Optimal solution and equity justified by clear criteria	• Work occurs within functioning units such as teams, organizations, countries • Known, hierarchical authority and responsibility • Risks are spatially and temporally proximate	• Social identities • Values • Personality • Disciplines • Professions • Politics • Cultures • Languages	• Moderate uncertainty allows cause–effect predictions • Predictability allows manageability • Risks are identifiable • Closed system limits interdependency on outside factors and increases control

are overwhelmed, disoriented, and don't know where to start, so crisis leadership often focuses on providing clear, short-term direction that treats symptoms (e.g., restores public safety) rather than treating underlying causes (e.g., reducing greenhouse gas emissions to mitigate the climate change that caused the extreme flooding). A crisis may require a style of leadership associated with command, where a single person or central authority can quickly mobilize resources to address immediate threats and give clarity to chaos. The Anthropocene, regrettably, is creating more crises, such as health pandemics, stronger hurricanes, disrupted food supplies, and life-threatening urban smog.

Many readers may be familiar with Rittel and Webber's classic work describing the attributes of wicked problems. Their work has been extended by Ronald Heifitz, Bryan Norton, and Keith Grint, three

Table 4.5. Attributes of Crisis Problems

Problem definition	Scales across which stakeholders must connect	Diversity across which stakeholders must collaborate	Uncertainties to which stakeholders must adapt
• Severe, immediate, obvious threat to health and well-being • Primary goal is to reduce uncertainty and chaos • Defined by someone in authority • Treat symptoms not causes	• Identifiable community of interest affected by the crisis • Highly centralized authority • Short time horizon	• Differences are temporarily set aside to address perceived large and shared threat • Defer to authority	• Extreme uncertainty • Stakeholders disoriented and don't know where to focus or start • Ignore aspects of problem not related to immediate health and security

authors who have informed our own work (Table 4.6).[3] Wicked problems, to paraphrase former UN secretary-general Kofi Annan, are "problems without passports." Their impacts cross geographic and political boundaries, and their solutions must as well. Also, because wicked problems are unique, no one has experience solving them; thus stakeholders' understanding of the problem will be changing as they learn more about it and while they simultaneously try to solve it. Many wicked problems are tragic in that someone or something will lose: win–win solutions don't exist. And solutions are hotly contested because no objective, external criterion exists by which to determine the best or optimal solution (e.g., people are trading off prosperity, identity, health, history, and biodiversity). The dynamism and uncertainty of wicked problems confound understanding, prediction, and control. Science, expertise, and technology may be of limited a priori use. Many wicked problems are

Table 4.6. Attributes of Wicked Problems

Problem definition	Scales across which stakeholders must connect	Diversity across which stakeholders must collaborate	Uncertainties to which stakeholders must adapt
WICKED			
• Iterative: engaging the problem changes stakeholder understanding, which changes the problem definition • Each situation unique • No optimal, calculated, objectively best outcome	• No one with authority over everyone who must be engaged • Open systems with unclear boundaries • Dispersed stakeholders • Multiscalar risks: local, regional, national, global • Tragedy of commons (individual rational actions don't lead to rational aggregate outcome) • Long time horizon	Tame, plus: • Contested: no win–win (someone loses) • Very diverse expertise needed • Transdisciplinary • Requires working well beyond existing institutions and arrangements	• High uncertainty • Unknown unknowns • Unpredictable, unclear cause–effect • Interventions cause ripples that create new problems • Dynamism requires continuous learning • Relentless: can't be solved, only improved or delayed • Requires continuous attention and learning
SUPER-WICKED			
Wicked, plus: • Slow, unseen impacts don't mobilize concern	Wicked, plus: • Key actors don't know they are involved	Wicked, plus: • Those who define the problem also cause it and thus must	Wicked, plus: • Immense and intimidating uncertainty about stake

continued on next page

Table 4.6. continued

Problem definition	Scales across which stakeholders must connect	Diversity across which stakeholders must collaborate	Uncertainties to which stakeholders must adapt
• Worsened by waiting • Will cause enormous harm and suffering if ignored • Interconnectedness with other problems necessitates designing to fail without bringing down the whole	• Key actors don't know or interact with one another • Risks increase with scale to create global tipping points	change to solve it • Extensively cross-sector • International, cross-cultural • Can't consult some stakeholders, such as future generations	holders, goals, system, and strategies • Accelerating, unpredictable, changing new conditions • Requires sense-making rather than problem solving

unsolvable, so failure is inevitable, and continuous effort and learning are required to address and mitigate them.

If these illustrative attributes of wicked problems aren't challenging enough, the second part of Table 4.6 explores attributes of what Kelly Levin and colleagues call super-wicked problems.[4] Climate change is a good example of a super-wicked problem. Everyone on Earth is both responsible and impacted: the people who cause the problem must solve it. These impacts and responsibilities are distributed unevenly and inequitably. Delay is not a good option because unknown tipping points might produce irreversible changes with potentially catastrophic consequences. Perhaps most confoundingly, deep interdependencies can cause unanticipated changes to ripple through local and global systems, ignoring geographic, political, and other boundaries, further changing conditions and people and causing further unanticipated changes that further amplify and extend impacts.

Hopefully you better understand why wicked problems are so vexing. Hopefully you also appreciate that this book attempts to go beyond understanding to action. It focuses on leadership practices that address wicked problems. Stated more strongly, most of the literature about wicked problems focuses on understanding the problem, we focus on actions that help respond to wicked problems and create new opportunities. Leadership practices for facilitating direction, alignment, and commitment in wicked situations are listed in Tables 4.1, 4.2, and 4.3 and described in detail in chapters 5, 6, and 7.

Conclusion

Many popular leadership theories and books focus on characteristics of leaders, such as charisma, that presumably depend on genetically determined personality or formative childhood experiences. Popular biographies of famous leaders typically follow a similar narrative: "leaders are born, not made." We disagree with the notion that preexisting personality types or childhood experiences determine your ability to practice or improve leadership. Leadership practices can be learned, and everyone can practice leadership from whatever position or job they happen to hold; hence this book.

When direction, alignment, and commitment exist, leadership occurs and things get accomplished. Fortunately, numerous leadership practices exist for facilitating direction, alignment, and commitment in the connective, collaborative, and adaptive conditions of wicked situations. We define and illustrate those practices in the remaining chapters of this book.

Hopefully you are feeling empowered. You can lead from where you are by facilitating direction, alignment, and commitment. Moreover, you can increase your influence and relevance by learning leadership skills and practices, such as those discussed next.

CHAPTER 5

Connecting across Space and Time

Connecting stakeholders across space and time is necessary if we are to respond effectively to the multiscalar, wicked situations of the Anthropocene. Stakeholders are so widely distributed, geographically and temporally, that many will never meet nor know one another. Still, actions must be coordinated. Key leadership practices for helping stakeholders connect and coordinate actions across space and time include the following:

- Accountability
- Storytelling
- Community of practice
- Train-the-trainer
- Scaling-up
- Diffusion
- Collective impact
- Social marketing

Accountability

"Sunshine is said to be the best of disinfectants" is a quote attributed to famed judge Louis Brandeis. It's a poetic phrase that captures the essence of accountability: people are connected when the consequences of their actions become visible to others. Actors causing harmful impacts are motivated to improve their practices to avoid shame and blame. Actors producing good outcomes are motivated to continue doing so by boosts to their reputations. Either way, people who don't know or don't meet one another are coordinating their actions: best practices for producing more sustainable outcomes get distributed through the system, and worst practices get sanctioned. This accountability strategy goes by other names, such as governance by disclosure, informational politics, and regulation by information.[1] It promotes shared direction because people must agree on what outcomes to report. It aligns action because people must work to produce those outcomes. It promotes commitment using reputational reward as motivations: shame and fame, leaders and laggards, rank and spank.

Accountability influences behavior in situations when people interact directly as well as when they are widely distributed. We focus on the latter because it is one of the few practices that work when actors are so widely dispersed that they likely will never encounter or directly negotiate with one another, and may not even realize they are connected.

Labeling, Certification, Standards, and Reporting

Product labeling provides perhaps the most familiar example. As consumers, we must navigate labels that signal organic and recycled ingredients, labor practices that are fair and respectful of human rights, agriculture that is free range and rainforest friendly, and products engineered to minimize energy and water use. Product labels, and the certification processes behind the labels, make sustainability impacts occurring at one part of the supply chain visible, not just to consumers but to people at other parts of the chain as well.

Demand for sustainable products from consumers and purchasing agents, enabled by accountability, was one of the market transformations discussed in chapter 2. More than one in every three consumers say they will buy products with a trusted label denoting sustainable best practices if price and quality are equal to similar but less sustainable products. Yet, in practice, most consumers are fickle and overloaded by information. Purchasing agents, in contrast, are paid and trained to guide their organization's purchasing. They are hardly fickle, and they do rely on certification and labels to inform their decisions. For example, a government agency may mandate that all new buildings meet certain energy efficient standards, and a chain of office supply stores may insist that the paper it sells is not linked to deforestation. Associations such as the Sustainable Purchasing Leadership Council help purchasing agents wade through the rising tide of information to make informed and influential decisions.

Industry standards are another example of accountability. Standards are developed by a coalition or "roundtable" of stakeholders, including producers, aggregators, consumers, and governmental and civil society organizations concerned about the impacts of market production systems. Producers agree to meet or exceed the standards and develop, apply, and share best practices for achieving those standards. Standards exist for most global commodities, including soybeans, beef, and palm oil. These standards address deforestation, pollution, labor rights, and other sustainability concerns. For example, CEOs of most major companies have pledged to abide by the United Nations Global Compact, which includes specific performance metrics related to human rights. The world's largest retailer, Walmart, provides another example of industry standards. It has committed to buying and selling products that meet sustainability standards which it develops and enforces.[2] Suppliers wanting to fill Walmart's shelves must demonstrate that they meet these standards, thereby further distributing those standards through global supply chains.

Sustainability reporting is another example of accountability. It is similar to product labels, except it doesn't target retail consumers. The reports allow motivated stakeholders to compare and contrast organizations based on their sustainability impacts. Many different reporting platforms exist, including CDP (formerly the Carbon Disclosure Project), GRI (the Global Reporting Initiative), and ISO (the International Organization for Standardization). The Sustainable Accounting Standards Board, for example, develops and promotes accounting metrics designed to help investors differentiate among companies based on sustainability-related factors that impact investment risk and return. Companies, therefore, are becoming more sustainable because accountability helps investors make more informed decisions. A case study of Host Hotels & Resorts is presented in chapter 13 of this book.

The examples discussed thus far focus mostly on market actors, but lots of other organizations use accountability practices to influence sustainability-related decisions and actions. World Resources Institute, the eminent nonpartisan environmental think tank, often deploys this strategy. Their strategic plan states, "We believe that access to transparent, decision-relevant information will drive more sustainable and equitable use of resources." Their Resource Watch program provides a great example. It is a free, simple-to-use web platform that helps governments, businesses, nongovernmental organizations, journalists, universities, and the general public examine, share, and use information about environmental changes, such as deforestation, as they happen. The hope is that actors will be motivated by reputation to use this information to influence behavior in real time.

A few more examples illustrate the widespread use of the accountability strategy. The US Federal Emergency Management Agency helps people assess the flood risk of a property before they build or buy; the

US Environmental Protection Agency's Safe Drinking Water Information System lets people examine the drinking water in their region; the National Oceanic and Atmospheric Administration (NOAA) Office for Coastal Management provides a Sea Level Rise Viewer that helps people visualize impacts of coastal flooding. And, perhaps the most widely known, the United Nations' Sustainable Development Goals encourage countries to report and compare themselves on metrics such as poverty, health, equality, governance, sustainable consumption, water, climate, and biodiversity.

Putting It into Practice

Accountability may be an effective way to coordinate action of dispersed actors, but doing it well is difficult and expensive. It requires reporting measures that matter (Table 5.1). Reporting formats need to be *accessible* to the people they are intended to influence. For example, in product labeling, information not available at the point of purchase requires consumers to use an app or internet search, which makes it less likely to be accessed and used to inform actual purchases. The information needs to be *material* to a stakeholder's decision. For example, if an investor wants to make a decision about a company, then reports about the quantity of greenhouse gases the company emits are much less relevant than reports about how those greenhouse gas emissions are related to profitability and risk. Measures also need to be *comprehensible*. Consumers and citizens struggle to understand reported technical details, such as tons of greenhouse gas emissions. Moreover, measures need to be *comparable* across choices the consumer or citizen is making. Again, using greenhouse gas emissions as an example, one company may report emissions per year, another may report emissions per product, another may report only emissions generated within the walls of the factory, while another may report emissions generated upstream in the supply chain from growing crops and generating electricity.

Table 5.1. Accountability Depends on Information Quality*

Material	Information must be meaningful and relevant to stakeholder decisions. That is, measure what matters.
Comparable	The information must allow stakeholders to compare choices.
Accessible	Information needs to be reported so that stakeholders can use it when they need to use it.
Comprehensible	Stakeholders must understand the information, so it can't be overly technical.
Actionable	The information needs to represent something that stakeholders can influence.
Affordable	The information must be updated frequently enough to inform stakeholders.
Benchmarked	Benchmarks can be used to evaluate progress and rate of change.
Precise Accurate Sensitive	These standard measurement qualities are critical: uncertainty and measurement error should be minimal; the measures should represent actual conditions; and as conditions change, so should the measures.

*Klaus Dingwerth and Margot Eichinger, "Tamed Transparency: How Information Disclosure under the Global Reporting Initiative Fails to Empower," *Global Environmental Politics* 10, no. 3 (2010): 74–96.

Accountability works best when actors responsible for causing and correcting impacts are concerned about naming, shaming, reputation, legitimacy, and/or social license to operate. These conditions are often not met. For example, many of the reports of the enormous greenhouse gas emissions associated with beef do not make it clear who is responsible: the rancher, the feedlot, the feed producer, the transporter, the slaughterhouse, the packager, the freezer, the chef, or the consumer. In addition, some actors are not vulnerable or receptive to the risk of reputational damage, typically because they are embedded up the supply chain and may not be visible to consumers or investors.

Problematically, the mechanism of accountability—sharing information—can be perverted to share disinformation and sow doubt.[3] Actors wanting to disrupt or delay accountability can confuse consumers, citizens, and other end users with misinformation, much as merchants-of-doubt confused and delayed action on climate and cigarettes. Accountability works only when the quality of information is trusted and trustworthy. Disclosing unreliable, poor-quality, or distorted information can overwhelm anyone trying to use that information.

Storytelling

It is not an exaggeration to say that stories change the world. People dispersed across great distances who don't know one another can coordinate their behavior when they believe in the same story. Yuval Harari, in *Sapiens: A Brief History of Humankind*, describes the human ability to collectively share a story as one of the few important features distinguishing human beings from other animals. The cognitive ability to share an abstraction facilitates cooperation among humans in large numbers, much larger than just families and tribes. Consider the impact of some of the world's megastories: free markets, money, trade, religion, corporations, nations, human rights, and sustainable development. Because people that have never met can share a nationality, a religion, or the belief that money has value, they can collaborate and cooperate in ways that transcend both geography and time. The stories about these abstract ideas influence behavior and organize society. But, as Harari notes, "Telling effective stories is not easy. The difficulty lies not in telling the story, but in convincing everyone else to believe it."

You may be tempted to dismiss "story" as something frivolous because you're thinking too narrowly, and conflating "story" with "excuse," "fairytale," or "fiction." Think more broadly. Humans are hardwired to know our world through story.[4] We use stories to tell others, and ourselves, who we are, where we came from, what we value, and why we do what we do. Stories order events, connect facts, and explain why things happen. No other species has this capacity to understand and coordinate behavior.

Stories perform several functions that promote direction, alignment, and commitment among people who are otherwise widely distributed and disconnected. Stories promote direction by explaining a goal, such as saving a species, spreading prosperity, or increasing innovation. Alignment is promoted when readers learn what the characters in the story do and how those actions can contribute to realizing the goal. Stories invite the reader to ask, "What can I do? What should I do?"[5] Commitment occurs when readers understand the motivation for the goals, the expected impacts of achieving them, and the reasons why sacrifices now will pay off in the future. Creating and telling a story, therefore, can not only connect people across time and space but also coordinate direction, alignment, and commitment among those who hear and read it, and possibly tell it again. Crafting and telling an effective story, however, is hard, and is perhaps more art than science. Fortunately, there are many guides and workshops for anyone interested.[6]

The following simple example illustrates how a story builds buy-in and commitment by helping people understand how their individual actions fit into something bigger and more meaningful:

A girl out for a walk came upon two women laboring in a field. The girl asked the first woman, whose slumping posture suggested she resented her work, "What are you doing?" To which she responded, "I am pulling weeds." The girl then asked the other worker, whose posture and humming suggested enthusiasm, "What are you doing?" The woman answered, "I am restoring habitat that will save a species!"[7]

Community of Practice and Learning

Communities of practice help people learn from their peers.[8] People with similar job responsibilities or professional positions do similar things, encounter similar challenges, and develop similar solutions, even though they work for different organizations or in different locations. By sharing lessons learned, they avoid reinventing the wheel and promote innovation. A community of practice will vet, improve, and share these lessons among people who otherwise wouldn't interact. Importantly, a community of practice can work when people are widely distributed by space and time and can only interact asynchronously or virtually.

Typically, a community of practice is not a method for coordinating a group of actors to agree on or implement actions but rather a method for building capacity in individuals who share similar practices to solve similar problems. With careful nurturing, however, the networks can become learning communities that enable members to interact, build one another's capacities, collectively reimagine shared problems, and even mobilize action.[9]

Once you know what to look for, you will find examples everywhere: your profession, a website or listserv, a support group within your business, and so on. The World Business Council for Sustainable Development is a community of practice comprising CEOs and corporate sustainability officers representing over 200 companies united by a desire to provide business leadership for sustainable development. Members learn from other leading companies, interact with other members, and gain access to a one-stop shop for tools and expertise to push their sustainability journey forward.

The International Union for Conservation of Nature (IUCN) is one of the largest and most diverse environmental networks, and it leverages communities of practice to promote learning, disseminate information, and share knowledge among its members. For example, its Rights-Based Approach community of practice shares case studies, publications, project information, and other resources to support the promotion and development of rights-based approaches to conservation worldwide.[10] Other IUCN communities of practice target surface freshwater, biodiversity and ecosystem services, large-scale marine protected areas, and the reduction of emissions from deforestation and forest degradation. Communities of practice also play a critical role in the World Bank's overall strategy in creating, sharing, and applying knowledge, with many forming to address knowledge gaps in a specific area.[11]

A famous example of a community of practice is one developed by and for Xerox customer service representatives who repair copy machines. The Xerox reps began exchanging tips and tricks at informal meetings and over breakfast or lunch. Xerox saw the value of these interactions and created a formal community of practice to increase interactions and shared lessons across the global network of representatives, using many of the attributes of successful communities of practice outlined in Table 5.2. It has been estimated that the improved practices benefited the corporation to the tune of approximately $100 million.[12]

A variant of community of practice, called learning networks, is illustrated in chapter 14 of this book, with the example of the Fire Learning Network promoting biodiversity and institutional change.

Successful communities of practice tend to be participatory rather than hierarchical, provide accessible and just-in-time learning, emphasize content and coaching relevant to practice, and be sufficiently funded and staffed. See Table 5.2 for explanations. Communities of practice exist in business, government, civil society, and everywhere in between. The Netweavers Network is a community of practice for people who design and manage networks to foster learning and adaptation; sort of a community of practice about communities of practice. You'll find lots of best practices on their website.[13]

Table 5.2. Attributes of Successful Communities of Practice (CoPs)

Participatory	CoPs are less hierarchical than academic degree programs or agency training workshops. They encourage autonomy, adaptability, self-coordination, and constructive peer review so that relationships reflecting mutual and shared everyday concerns can emerge.
Accessible	CoPs have multiple media for easy and accessible communication, sharing resources, and asking questions.
Relevant	Participants must see the CoP as contributing to their own work priorities in a mutually reinforcing way, as members share know-how and experiential knowledge about their successes and failures.
Funded and staffed	Sponsorship is critical for seed money and operating costs. Staff help ensure continuity over time and hold participants accountable. However, domination of the network by the sponsor or staff can lessen collective ownership, creativity, and self-direction, threatening the essence of the network approach.

Train-the-Trainer

This simple and familiar strategy can multiply your impact by creating a ripple effect, whereby people who receive training then train others, who then train others, and so on. As the familiar adage says, If you give someone a fish, you temporarily ease their hunger. If you teach them to fish, then they can feed themselves for a lifetime. If you teach them to teach others to fish, you help them create a fishing industry that raises living standards for their entire community.

The train-the-trainer strategy might be useful if you are a small organization with limited staff and budget and want to multiply your impact. It works best for well-understood problems like vegetable gardening, managing a local water supply, and installing solar energy systems. That is, the lessons that are taught need to be simple enough to be easily grasped, and generalizable enough to work in most situations without nuanced adaptation by a professional.

Examples abound of efforts that train people and encourage them to engage their communities and train others, such as Master Naturalist and Master Gardener programs operating throughout the United States. The third section of this book presents a detailed example of a small organization working in poor, rural villages in India that uses this technique to build capacity in women. By equipping participating women with leadership and financial skills (which may be as simple as managing a bank account) and encouraging them to apply those skills in their communities, it often produces dramatic improvements in quality of life.

The train-the-trainer process is intuitive: identify people, train them, and support their efforts to train others. Yet all three facets present challenges. People must be selected that have capacity and status in their communities to influence others, otherwise they will be ineffective at passing forward what they learned. Training must include, in addition to technical tools, the skills to teach and motivate others. Teaching participants how to teach and motivate others can be more difficult than teaching them how to use technical tools.

Successful training networks require monitoring: quality control is needed to protect the brand, and feedback is needed to make revisions. Successful training networks often provide periodic opportunities to gather the trainers together. Conferences and retreats help trainers recharge, and they motivate commitment by acknowledging work well done and celebrating shared identity. A simple internet search for train-the-trainer manuals or guides will turn up plenty of useful resources.

Scaling-Up

Scaling-up helps replicate and spread isolated innovations so they have large, system-wide impact.[14] It differs from communities of practice and train-the-trainer, discussed in the preceding sections, which generally spread simple knowledge and technical expertise through a defined region or type of work. Scaling-up is required for more complex projects whose success depends not just on knowledge but also on partnerships, innovation, funding, and politicking. Consider an entrepreneur who creates a profitable solar energy venture, or a nonprofit organization that captures food waste and feeds hungry people. These innovations involve multiple people and organizations disrupting business as usual, and innovating new relationships and practices that have meaningful impacts for the people they reach. But, without scaling-up, they produce mere drops in the bucket compared to the scale of change that is possible and necessary.

Let's take a closer look at a food waste example. As noted in chapter 2's discussion of Anthropocene challenges, agriculture is responsible for greenhouse gas emissions, aquifer depletion, pollution, and lost habitat. It is not unusual for 25 percent of a region's food supply to be wasted, so waste reduction efforts can be consequential. Some food gets wasted simply because it is ugly. Finicky consumers will not purchase oddly shaped or blemished fruit and vegetables, so they get sorted into trash or left to rot in the fields. But innovators are figuring out how to get ugly vegetables to people who are more hungry than picky, or, with a bit of processing, to transform them into tasty juices and other products whose value does not depend on appearance. These enterprises generate profits, employ staff, improve diets, and reduce food waste—a win–win–win–win. We need more of them if we hope to make a dent in the enormous and widespread challenge of feeding a more prosperous and populated world. Reducing waste from one farm, sorting shed, or grocery store won't have much impact on the larger challenge; to make a larger impact requires scaling-up.

A formal process exists for scaling-up an innovation. Begin by differentiating between the work leading to the innovation (discussed in chapter 7) and the work needed to scale-up that innovation (discussed here). Many innovations are difficult to scale because their initial success depends on unique local conditions, such as a charismatic leader, a preexisting social network, or unique economic or environmental conditions. Evidence that the innovation works is different than evidence of its scalability, so additional information must be collected, monitored, and analyzed to explore scalability.

Consider whether the right people are involved. The people and organizations best suited to innovate may not be best at scaling. Innovators need the courage and insight to test an idea and to generate energy through acts of creation. They possess the capacity to fail frequently and pivot quickly. Scaling, in contrast, can be more methodical and longer term, requiring different processes and personalities.

Larry Cooley and colleagues at Management Systems International have been a go-to consultancy for scaling efforts. In the spirit of scaling-up, they have developed, tested, applied, and shared best practices, case studies, and training tools for scaling. Much of the Table 5.3 checklist is derived from these resources. Other guides are listed in the notes.[15]

Diffusion

Diffusion theory and practices provide another powerful strategy for connecting and aligning stakeholder behavior.[16] They are often applied in the health and agriculture professions where innovations of medicine or farming need to be adopted by countless actors before meaningful, system-wide change occurs. In treating diabetes, for example, a behavior change must be adopted not just by hospitals and doctors but by nurses, insurance companies, nutritionists, and of course the patients themselves.

This section reviews two key characteristics that apply to most diffusion efforts: (1) the characteristics of the innovations that make them more likely to be adopted and diffused through a network and (2) the

Table 5.3. Scalability Check Sheet

Attribute	Characteristics of more scalable projects
Impact	• Addresses specific perceived needs of the target population • Delivers large, observable benefits to many people
Acceptability	• Minimal change required in social/cultural practices and minimal opposition to that change • Strategies consistent with government and other organizations
Champions	• Powerful advocates supporting innovation and scaling
Constituency	• Strong and growing demand for change/innovation
Simplicity	• Simple and easily understood explanation of how action will lead to change • Few decision points • Few actions and partners to coordinate
Alignment	• Key stakeholders know their roles
Management Capacities	• Identified lead organization supporting transition from demonstration to scaling • Requisite skills to implement innovation exist in-network
Accountability	• Clear metrics • Method for monitoring and sharing to evaluate progress
Financial Viability	• Low cost • Relies on existing infrastructure • Self-financing, commercially viable, and/or commitment to public financing

characteristics of the people who are more or less likely to adopt and diffuse an innovation through a network.

Five characteristics of innovations influence the likelihood that it will be adopted. These factors are similar to the attributes of innovations that are easily scaled up, discussed in the previous section (see Table 5.3). You should design your innovation and your promotion of the innovation with these characteristics in mind:

- Clear relative advantage: The new idea/behavior produces clear benefits that are better than the idea, program, or behavior it replaces. The advantage can be increased with tax breaks or direct payments that share costs of adopting the innovation.
- Compatibility: The innovation is consistent with the norms, values, experiences, and needs of the potential adopters. It needs to fit the culture and the economy. It needs to be something that adopters have the training, strength, and time to do.
- Complexity: The innovation is easy to understand, use, or do. Explanations must reflect local traditions, language, and tools.
- Trialability: The innovation can be tested and tried, without great risk or expense, before a commitment to adopt is made.
- Observability: The benefits/impacts can be seen or otherwise made tangible.

In addition to making the innovation easy to adopt, you need to design a strategy for introducing and spreading it through the network of people whom you want to adopt it. People differ in their receptivity to innovations and thus differ in how they should be introduced to the innovation. Diffusion theory segments people into five groups that help you plan diffusion efforts (Table 5.4).

Adoption typically spreads from the innovators to the early adopters and then on to early majority, late majority, and even laggards. Therefore, it makes sense to sequence diffusion efforts: first get the innovators on board, then target the early adopters, and so on. Importantly, each population segment is receptive to different strategies promoting adoption. Innovators, for instance, are receptive to experts and other innovators from outside the network: they go looking for new ideas they can bring back and apply in their location. For the same reason, innovators will be less receptive to opinion leaders within their community who innovators assume are championing established ideas, not innovations.

Table 5.4. Market Segments of Innovation Adopters

Segment	Characteristics	How to motivate
Innovators	Risk takers, often younger, often cosmopolitan and/or more connected to diverse cultures, experts, and innovators outside their core network. They are secure enough in finance and status to be resilient in the face of failure.	Receptive to external credential and expertise. Demotivated by friends, relatives, and opinion leaders internal to the network.
Early adopters	Motivated to succeed or advance socially and professionally. Slightly more risk averse than innovators. These may be opinion leaders of a network.	Influenced by near peers and familiar, trusted information sources, defensible information, and demonstration of benefits.
Early majority	People who don't like to lead or take risk but are willing to follow. Open to but slower to change. Have above average social status and some contact with early adopters.	Testimonials from early adopters. Strong examples of success, by using case studies, free samples, and success stories.
Late majority	People who have scarce resources, abhor change, or will wait until they see verifiable proof that the innovation works, and perhaps risk falling behind if they don't adopt the change.	User testimonials, hard data and statistics, and peer pressure from the other four categories. They need clear evidence that most other people have tried the innovation and approve of it.
Laggards	People who stick to their methods and routines out of tradition and identity. Tend to be advanced in age, lowest social status, and lowest financial capacity to respond to being wrong.	May change only if there is no other option. These individuals typically have an aversion to change agents. Only persuaded by family and close friends.

Early adopters and early majority, however, are receptive to local opinion leaders. So once you have the innovators on board, you should then target well-respected and well-connected people in the community/network of interest and get them to promote the innovation. Their status and standing in the community will give credibility to the innovation. It does not make sense to target those in the late majority or laggards until you have the early majority on board, and even then the only way to get laggards on board will be if close family and friends become advocates for the innovation—trying to persuade late majority and laggards with testimonials from internal or external change agents may be counterproductive. When promoting an innovation, try to assess where the adoption is on the spectrum and who needs to be targeted with what message and by what person and media. Be wise with your time and resources, and get the right influencers and media on board at the right time. Get to know them and their concerns and what it will take for them to adopt and promote the innovation.

Collective Impact

Collective impact is a set of best practices for organizing multiple stakeholders dispersed throughout a region, watershed, or city, so that their coordinated impact exceeds, by far, the sum of their isolated and piecemeal efforts. As an example, consider the challenge of getting a city to reduce its greenhouse gas emissions—which is key if we are to mitigate climate change. Doing so requires fundamentally restructuring how a city functions. Isolated, piecemeal efforts will have a negligible impact.

In chapter 11, we examine how a city used collective impact to coordinate and connect numerous factors needed to significantly reduce its carbon footprint. For example, to reduce emissions from transportation, the city needed to provide mass transit, which in turn required increasing residential density, infrastructure, and mixed-use development to support walking, buses, trams, and trains, and shopping and working near home. The city also needed ride-sharing programs, more efficient vehicles, electric charging stations, bike racks and bike lanes, and showers at work for sweaty bikers. It also needed to reduce emissions from its own fleet. Similar extensive and intertwined coordination was needed for building construction, power generation, and so on. Progress on matters this complicated requires countless actors dispersed over a large area coordinating their actions without even meeting or knowing they were coordinated—collective impact provided the framework for coordinating these actions.

For many wicked challenges, single, isolated efforts by individual organizations or small partnerships are ineffective, no matter how well intentioned, innovative, and resourced. Meaningful impact requires coordination of numerous stakeholders attacking numerous underlying issues in numerous ways, simultaneously, in the same place or in multiple places at once, repeatedly, for a long time. These stakeholders are unlikely to know each other or to have worked together previously, and some may even be competitors in other instances because they provide similar services to similar clients.

There are excellent resources and consultancies that teach and guide collective impact efforts.[17] Most successful collective impact efforts have the following five characteristics: trusted process and common agenda, mutually reinforcing activities, shared measurement, continuous communication, and backbone support (Table 5.5). It is reassuring to note that the theory of shared leadership—direction, alignment, commitment—is clearly evidenced in these five sets of best practices. Direction is achieved by developing an agenda that is shared and measurements that clearly define objectives. Alignment is promoted through aligning mutually reinforcing activities. Commitment is promoted by continuous communication and shared measurements that hold everyone accountable. Backbone support is probably the most overlooked component of

Table 5.5. Keys to Successful Collective Impact

Condition	Practice
Trusted process and common agenda	Agree to a process that leads to a shared understanding of the challenge and to the strategies needed to address it.
Mutually reinforcing activities	Coordinate differentiated activities by diverse actors.
Shared measurement	Measure and report progress on goals to facilitate learning, improvement, and accountability.
Continuous communication	All players engage in frequent and structured open communication to build trust, ensure mutual objectives, create common motivation, hold one another accountable, and learn from mistakes and successes.
Backbone support	Provide funds and staff to support operations, including meeting management, proposal writing, and data collection and management.

collective impact, and hence a reason why multistakeholder efforts often fail. Some organization or group of organizations needs to provide the dedicated staff and infrastructure to support the process that aligns and organizes stakeholders.

Social Marketing

You've probably been at a strategy meeting where someone suggested an information campaign: "If people just knew more about the problem, then they would change their behaviors." Unfortunately, it is exceedingly difficult to change, let alone coordinate, people's activities just by giving them information. Information alone rarely changes behavior; thus information campaigns can waste time and resources that could be used in more effective strategies. There are many reasons why information is ineffective (discussed in chapter 6), including confirmation bias, identity protective reasoning, filter bubbles, and echo chambers.

Table 5.6. Keys to Successful Social Marketing Campaigns

Tactic	Explanation
Remove barriers to behavior	Even if you successfully convince people to change behavior, they often can't because of limited time, money, control, know-how, and countless other barriers. It often takes policy or structural change to remove these barriers. For example, people might want to walk or bike to work but can't because they live too far away.
Target one-time versus repetitive behaviors	The impact of an information campaign is likely short-lived, so target behaviors that have lasting impacts. For example, target purchasing an energy-efficient car or appliance rather than everyday commuting or dishwashing behavior.
Use commitment strategies	Simply signing a pledge triggers commitment and changes behavior when it is coupled with information about why behavior should change.
Offer token incentives	Token incentives have large impacts, such as paying an extra half a penny to use plastic bags or several cents on a bottle deposit.
Target specific behaviors	Avoid broad suggestions such as "reduce your carbon footprint." Use specific, context-relevant suggestions such as "avoid meat consumption one day per week."
Make individuals believe they can make a difference	Apathy kicks in and motivations wane when people believe their behaviors make trivial impacts. Leave no question that individual action matters.

Social marketing is a method devised to make information campaigns more effective. It has been developed and tested in efforts targeting cigarette smoking, sexually transmitted disease, and littering. Social marketing requires large, well-funded, highly coordinated efforts to change norms and remove barriers.

This section seeks to caution you about simple information campaigns and to introduce some of the key tactics of social marketing so you can evaluate whether it is a good fit for your situation. Key tactics from the extensive literature on social marketing are summarized in Table 5.6.[18]

Conclusion

Leadership for sustainable development in the Anthropocene requires creative tools for tackling challenges whose causes, impacts, risks, and actors are widely distributed over space and time. It requires connecting stakeholders who may never meet or know one another, and coordinating disparate activities to have large-scale and system-wide impacts. Fortunately, there are strategies to address these challenges, such as those reviewed in this chapter.

Unfortunately, the wickedness of the Anthropocene presents more than distributed challenges. We must also find ways to collaborate across polarizing and mounting differences that divide stakeholders, and maintain progress by adapting to change in the face of confounding uncertainty and repeated failure. The next two chapters explore collaborative and adaptive leadership practices that address these other aspects of wicked challenges.

CHAPTER 6

Collaborating across Differences

No profession, discipline, business, government, community, or nation possesses sufficient vision and resources to address the wicked situations of the Anthropocene. Collaboration is required. Diverse stakeholders must be engaged. Unfortunately, facilitating direction, alignment, and commitment is difficult when stakeholders hold different identities, agendas, factual beliefs, worldviews, and values. This chapter focuses on specific strategies that can enable collaboration across differences. These leadership practices are also very useful in tame and crisis situations.

- Pick your battles.
- Use facts cautiously.
- Manage identity.
- Navigate differences.
- Build and repair trust.
- Form partnerships.

Before discussing these strategies, it is necessary to explain characteristics of human psychology that can hamper collaboration.

Psychological Challenges

People come preloaded with hardware and software that complicate collaborating across differences. This section reviews several of the most challenging: elephant riding, confirmation bias, filter bubbles, identity protective reasoning, and echo chambers.

Elephant Riding

Jonathan Haidt, in *The Righteous Mind: Why Good People Are Divided by Politics and Religion,* uses the metaphor of an elephant and a rider to explain the current best scientific understanding of a human's decision-making system, a metaphor we will use throughout this chapter.[1] The *elephant* is evolutionarily older, emotional, instinctive, hormonal, and precognitive. It makes decisions quickly to steer us away from threats and toward rewards. The elephant's *rider* represents conscious rational thinking—the voice in your head. It is more recently evolved, self-referential, consciously accessible, slower, and shareable, and it requires lots of attentional resources and gets easily fatigued and distracted.

The elephant makes 99 percent of your decisions, and then the rider justifies them. The elephant acts quickly, using limited information, stereotypes, assumptions, preconceptions, and emotions. Once the elephant starts leaning toward a decision, the rider tends to follow in the same direction and to look for reasons to justify that direction.

Most people assume that they carefully and logically analyze the costs, benefits, and other evidence to decide what is in their own best interests before they make a decision. But psychological science now refutes that assumption. People rarely use analytical thinking to inform and make a decision; instead, we use rational thinking to justify decisions already made by our emotional and intuitive brain (Table 6.1). To paraphrase Hume: reason serves emotion.

Humans are wired this way. The default setting on our reasoning

Table 6.1. Three Types of Rational Thinking

Analytical thinking (rider)	Unusual: rational, careful, logical analysis of costs, benefits, evidence, and logic to evaluate what is in our best interests before we make a decision
Justification thinking (rider)	Usual: rational, careful, logical justification of decisions after we make a decision
Quick, emotional, instinctual thinking (elephant)	Usual: quick decisions that require limited time and energy and thus use limited information, stereotypes, and preconceptions that have worked well in the past to steer us away from threats and toward rewards

mechanism (our rider) is to justify ourselves so that we make sense and look good to ourselves and others. We use our reasoning to pursue egotistical and socially strategic goals, such as promoting our reputation and convincing others to support our side in disputes. To use an analogy suggested by Haidt, our rider works more like a lawyer arguing a case than a scientist seeking truth. The lawyer's job is to win the client's case, whether the facts say the client is guilty or innocent. Evolution selected for this trait. Gossip, status, likeability, and peer evaluation determined who had access to resources and mates, just as they do today. Ancestors who could convince others, and themselves, of their legitimacy are the ones who thrived, reproduced, and passed on to us the genes that wire our brains for justification thinking. Overconfidence is a common result. Most people deceive themselves and systematically overestimate their skills. The implications are manifold and well documented, including tournament entry decisions, CEO behavior, self-control problems, and overestimation of generosity and selflessness.

The human tendency toward justification thinking may be a blow to your ego if you've assumed that you use facts to make cold, calculated, analytical decisions. Accept it. Know yourself, know the limitations of how you think, and know that others have the same limitations. Human reasoning is not designed to find truth in a situation but rather to protect and enhance ego and social standing. We are all really good at riding elephants. Strategies discussed later in this chapter use this tendency to promote collaboration.

Confirmation Bias (and Filter Bubbles)

Humans are surprisingly gullible. We will believe most anything that makes us appear consistent and reasonable and that justifies our elephant's quick decisions. We easily recall facts that support past decisions and actively suppress memories that don't. For example, a heavy coffee drinker will look for and remember evidence that confirms caffeine is not linked to health risks, and a climate change skeptic will find and remember instances when climate science has changed and conclude it is often wrong. Frustratingly, even if you do manage to convince someone with your facts, they are likely, as time passes, to suppress and not recall facts that don't support their position, so all your hard work will be for naught.

Confirmation bias explains why anecdotes are so powerful: people remember one instance that confirms their expectations and emphasize it over all other information. Confirmation bias also explains why you are unlikely to change someone's mind with facts. Their riders tend to ignore facts that don't support their elephant's decisions and instead focus on facts that do.

Filter bubbles support confirmation bias. They feed you information that supports your positions and filter out contrary information. Internet search engines personalize your requests based on what you liked and clicked in the past. You subscribe to news feeds that support your assumptions, and you receive information from sources that you like. You socialize with like-minded people who find and share information that reinforces your shared biases. Don't feel bad; everybody does it.

The resulting filter bubble puts confirmation bias on steroids. People sharing a filter bubble generate and share information that reinforces their worldview. Over time, the self-reinforcing feedback creates a distinct worldview that no longer intersects with the worldview of people in another filter bubble.[2] The result is that people focus on different facts, interpret facts differently, and don't validate their facts outside their filter bubble. Different, isolated understandings of the world emerge, making collaboration across different filter bubbles nearly impossible because collaboration requires sharing an understanding of the situation. Identity protective reasoning and echo chambers make collaborating across differences even more difficult.

Identity Protective Reasoning (and Echo Chambers)

You likely use identity protective reasoning whenever you engage in justification thinking (see Table 6.1), which is most of the time.[3] You can't escape it. Evolutionary pressures selected for it. Humans are social animals. Recognizing and cooperating with members of one's group enhanced reproductive success, as did recognizing and being cautious of out-group members who could harm your group and your offspring. We are evolutionarily predisposed to quickly distinguish in-group from out-group members. We identify with and protect the group to which we belong. During humanity's evolutionary journey, when evolution selected for this trait, the groups we identified with were family and tribe. Now we identify with groups defined by political party, citizenship, gender orientation, educational background, and favorite media outlet. Example topics that signal group affiliation and trigger identity protective reasoning include guns, homosexuality, global trade, abortion, sustainability, government regulation, religion, taxes, and climate change.

Let's use climate change as an example. Climate triggers identity protective reasoning in both climate action skeptics and climate action advocates. Let's imagine the mind of a skeptic when talking to a climate action advocate. At the first mention of climate change, rather than focusing on facts being presented, the skeptic hears their internal voice—their rider—reinforcing core beliefs and values of the identity they feel is under threat. For example, the skeptic's inner voice will be arguing that the person explaining climate science is an out-of-touch, overeducated elitist who disregards the value of hard-working citizens; that God has dominion over the Earth and humans can't change climate, and to argue otherwise is blasphemy; that government is already too big, and solutions to climate change such as cap-and-trade will make government bigger and even more of a threat to national security; that existing government regulations already stifle business innovation and decrease market efficiencies, which will threaten retirement savings and harm America's future, and so on. None of the climate action advocate's facts were "heard." The climate skeptic just rehearsed and reinforced preexisting beliefs.

Perversely, more highly educated people tend to be better at identity protective reasoning because they are better trained to marshal the facts and arguments that they and others in their group can then use to defend their group's identity and positions. Jerry Taylor, for example, is a really smart person who was once a climate skeptic. In fact, he is so smart about climate that the Cato Institute, a leading conservative think tank, employed him as a spokesperson for climate skepticism. He offers a rare example of someone changing his mind on climate. He did so, not because he was persuaded by facts, but because his identity was less about being a political conservative/climate skeptic than it was about being a smart, independent, critical adviser to policy makers. He changed his mind and became an advocate for climate action when he realized that he was misrepresenting the science and economics of climate change. In an interview describing his transformation, he describes how he effectively and selectively constructed arguments consistent with his group and was "motivated to hold a tribal line."[4]

Echo chambers amplify identity protective reasoning. An echo chamber actively undermines anyone who disagrees with community doctrine or threatens group identity. Dissenting voices are not just actively excluded, as in the case of a filter bubble; they are actively discredited. Again, take climate change as an example. A climate skeptic pays no immediate price for being skeptical about climate science; there is little one person can do to affect climate change, so the consequences are small if someone misinterprets climate science and doesn't act according to climate activists' suggestions. In contrast, if a climate skeptic expresses openness to climate action arguments, then the risk is high that they will suffer devastating social consequences, including loss of trust, status, and economic opportunities—they will be expelled, shunned, and actively shamed by other skeptics. For example, when conservative South Carolina congressman Bob Ingles came out in support of climate action, he was subjected to scathing critiques by conservative commentators, lost his next election, and is now on the fringe of the Republican party.

Identity protective reasoning fueled by echo chambers creates a major barrier to collaboration because, in combination, they cause people to actively discredit and systematically undermine anybody in their group who appears open to alternative views.[5] People offering alternative facts and logic are seen as untrustworthy, dangerous, and unworthy of collaboration. The echo chamber actively discredits opponents and rewards discrediting, creates feedback loops that strengthen the chamber's boundaries, ravages any contrary information that might get through, and threatens anyone who questions the group's dogma. Worse, it creates intolerance of collaboration and compromise because collaboration becomes working with the enemy, and compromise becomes conceding to the enemy.

People are prewired in ways that complicate collaborating across differences. The rest of this chapter offers targeted strategies for dealing with these complications.

Pick Your Battles

Be strategic about stakeholder engagement. Some people will be difficult, if not impossible, to collaborate with, no matter how sophisticated your toolbox. Some differences are too vast to bridge, and some thinking is too entrenched to change. In the next section we explain a counterintuitive strategy: consider targeting elites, even though they will be the most invested, informed, and equipped to resist and refute your efforts. Then we explain that even this may be wasted effort because of network propaganda loops. Our purpose here, in raising these points, is to help you focus your energies on tasks and people that have a good chance of success.

Target Elites

Identity protective reasoning explains why people respond to identity and reputation more than to facts. It also suggests that the best educated, most informed, and most invested stakeholders are going to have tons of facts and logic at their disposal to defend their positions—they will be able to go toe-to-toe with the best informed experts on the "other" side, making for tedious, arcane, difficult conversations. Yet—and here is the conundrum—it may make sense to target them, rather than people who are undecided and less informed.

People who don't know the facts may not have the time or ability to dig into the nuances of the issue. They adopt the positions held by the elites of their social group who do have the time and ability to wade through the difficult details of issues that affect their group. For example, a person skeptical of climate action may not want to learn about climate science, no matter how motivated you are to teach them. They are skeptical of climate change, not because of factual ignorance, but because they identify with a group that opposes climate action. The only way to change their mind is to change the position of their group:

if the elites change positions, so will the others. This means you need to persuade the group's leadership, which means engaging the best educated and most informed people on the other side. Buckle up!

Network Propaganda Loops

Not all stakeholders are willing or able to collaborate. In their book *Network Propaganda: Manipulation, Disinformation, and Radicalization in American Politics*, Benkler and colleagues suggest that 25–30 percent of the US public are trapped in network propaganda loops, and you will not be able to effectively communicate or collaborate with them unless you join their networks. In other words, tens of millions of people in the US may be essentially unreachable to you (we assume, because you are reading this book, that you are not embedded in one of these loops). If this situation is as significant as the study suggests, and these feedback loops do not change, then you will need to plan your influence strategies accordingly. It may require working around, rather than directly with, a large portion of the population.

Benkler and colleagues argue that network propaganda loops—created by Twitter, Facebook, and the rest of the media ecosystem—reinforce confirmation bias, identity protective reasoning, filter bubbles, and echo chambers. These self-reinforcing feedback loops promote partisan propaganda and divide people. To accurately convey this troubling finding, we quote Benkler and colleagues extensively.

Two large media ecosystems exist: the far right and everybody else. "The American media ecosystem consists of two distinct, structurally different media ecosystems. One part is the right-wing, dominated by partisan media outlets that are densely interconnected and insular and anchored by Fox News and Breitbart. The other part spans the rest of the spectrum. It includes outlets from the left to historically center-right publications like the *Wall Street Journal* and is anchored by media organizations on the center and center-left that adhere to professional standards of journalism. There is no distinct left-wing media ecosystem that parallels the right in its internal coherence or insularity from the center."

The two media ecosystems operate differently. The "everybody else" media ecosystem, hereafter called mainstream media, operates using journalistic norms, developed in the twentieth century, that call for media to self-police based on fact checking. Investigative scoops are lauded and falsehoods shamed. These norms slow the spread of partisan statements that are demonstrably false; that is, they hinder the spread of propaganda. "This does not suggest that the center and left are always error-free or pure of heart." Indeed, Benkler and colleagues document plenty of partisanship and errors in mainstream media reporting. But dynamics in the far right media ecosystem, in contrast, "tend to reinforce partisan statements, irrespective of their truth, and to punish actors—be they media outlets or politicians and pundits—who insist on speaking truths that are inconsistent with partisan frames and narratives dominant within the ecosystem." That is, the mainstream media ecosystem self-corrects based on whether reports conform to facts, while the far right media ecosystem self-corrects based on whether reports conform to ideology—it supports the spread of propaganda. "Partisan falsehoods thrive on the right not as errors but as design features of the network . . . and . . . have made the right-wing ecosystem a richer breeding ground and receptive ecosystem for propagandist efforts, foreign and domestic." This finding suggests that no amount of fact checking or fact sharing by mainstream media will persuade people in the far right media ecosystem: other strategies will be needed in order to connect and collaborate with them.

Both media systems have self-reinforcing feedback loops powered by the self-interests of the public, media outlets, advertisers, and politicians. The public engage their respective media ecosystems because they want to know what is going on in the world and how their political leaders are doing, "but [they] also want to get information that confirms them in their worldview and identity." That is, identity protective reasoning motivates people to "seek out confirming information, reject or discount disconfirming evidence, and to do otherwise requires hard cognitive and emotional work. . . . They look for media outlets and politicians that will inform them as best as possible without suffering too much cognitive discomfort." The media, in order to make money or have impact, seek to build a large audience by attracting the public. Thus they need to provide what people want, creating a feedback loop that reports on topics that reinforce their audiences' worldview and identity. "This involves interactions between reporters, editors, and owners, all of whom themselves operate under motivated reasoning and are perfectly able to lie to themselves to reduce the tensions between their often conflicting goals."

Politicians and advertisers support a similar feedback loop because, to reach an audience, they need to deliver a message within one of those distinct ecosystems, which means they have to echo the audience's language, logic, and values, which forms a feedback loop that reinforces that language, logic and values. "Although politicians find ways to reach out directly to their constituents, they must work through media outlets to reach a larger public. Politicians must also be informed both about the state of the world and about their voters' perceptions of the state of the world, and must balance between these goals when they are in tension. For this purpose, politicians consume the media their voters do."

The two media systems rarely intersect, and thus are insular and becoming increasingly distinct. Collaboration among people from different media ecosystems is exceedingly difficult and, pragmatically, you might want to assess stakeholders and decide whether collaboration is even worth trying. Troublingly, if we all stop trying, the divisions of today may only widen.

What can you do, other than be aware of the forces impacting how you and others understand the world? Not much. You can look for ways to break out of filter bubbles and echo chambers that the media feed-back loops accentuate. But that only impacts you, not stakeholders you need to collaborate with. Benkler and colleagues suggest ways to tame the network propaganda feedback loops, but they admit that the current toolbox is limited. New tools need to be developed.

However, in situations where stakeholders are open to potential collaboration, many useful tools already exist to promote it. Let's turn our attention there.

Use Facts Cautiously

Facts aren't required for collaboration to occur. Direction, alignment, and commitment can be built on fiction, faith, myth, ideals, intuitions, and misperceptions. Nonetheless, most sustainability professionals—the authors of this book included—believe that facts are necessary. We believe humanity is more likely to navigate the wicked challenges of the Anthropocene if direction, alignment, and commitment are constructed using the best available facts.

Unfortunately, due to aspects of human psychology reviewed earlier in the chapter, people are capable of remarkable rationalizations to justify their decisions, and mostly ignore, invent, or selectively attend to facts. Moreover, the mere mention of some facts can be counterproductive if doing so triggers identity protective reasoning. Keeping these cautions in mind, this section introduces tactics for using facts effectively.

- Agree on criteria.
- Use joint fact finding.
- Make conflict useful.
- Clarify conflict.
- Frame the facts.
- Use images and graphics.

Agree on Criteria

This suggestion makes admittedly weak tea, but needs mentioning. Would-be collaborators must mutually accept that confirmation bias, identity protective reasoning, filter bubbles, and echo chambers exist, and distort the information they rely on. If people accept these limitations and tendencies of their brain, then it might be possible to get them to agree to standards of evidence—something more rigorous than internet searches—that make facts credible. Perhaps most usefully, encourage collaborators to agree on using facts that can be falsified with experience and observation. If collaborators use only vague assertions that can't be falsified, then they are encouraging confirmation bias because nothing will be able to refute their assertions. More controversially, get stakeholders to agree to use facts from nonpartisan research groups, such as the Congressional Research Service or peer-reviewed scientific journals (unfortunately, these sources are increasingly controversial because they are seen as partisan).

Use Joint Fact Finding

Groups collaborating to make decisions about wicked situations face imperfect and often contradictory information and may end up mired in identity protective reasoning fueled by dueling scientists: each side marshaling the facts that best advance their interests and discrediting the contradictory facts others provide. As Thomas Sowell phrased it, "For every expert, there is an equal and opposite expert." Joint fact finding offers one way forward, albeit one that is a bit laborious and requires a trained facilitator.[6] It calls upon stakeholders and technical experts to work together, not out of altruism, but as a means to generate outcomes that all parties find acceptable. Stakeholders must begin the process early and stay engaged. They must jointly identify the information needed to make the decision and agree on and engage experts that they trust to help find and/or conduct research that provides that information. This process works best in situations where there are disagreements about information, low levels of trust among participants, and sufficient resources to fund facilitators and fact finders. It is less appropriate when there are significant power imbalances among stakeholders and the facilitated process cannot be convened.

Make Conflict Useful

Even though confirmation bias limits our ability to critique our own rationale, it makes us really good at poking holes in the rationale used by others. As a result, a group composed of diverse people, properly managed, tends to produce better decisions than a group composed of similar people because the diverse group's members question one another's reasoning and assumptions. A homogeneous group confirms one another's assertions using confirmation bias and, worse, may become an echo chamber that vilifies sources of information they disagree with. This relationship between group diversity and decision quality presents a paradox for long-term collaborative efforts (Figure 6.1). The diversity of experiences within a group that produces better decisions can also cause dysfunction if people think their identities are under attack. Hence high-functioning groups likely need explicit processes for managing conflict.[7]

To use conflict constructively, a group can intentionally create a time for critiquing and questioning ideas so people can be alert to mitigating feelings of identity threat; that is, help people recognize that a critique of their idea is not intended to critique them personally but instead intended to improve the group's decision. The purpose of comments made during this time would be different than during times when supportive, brainstorming comments are expected. Role-playing also works. If people know that someone is playing the role of devil's advocate or critic, then the criticism is more likely to be interpreted as questioning the idea and not attacking the person who offered the idea. Perhaps most importantly, collaborators need to be coached to expect and

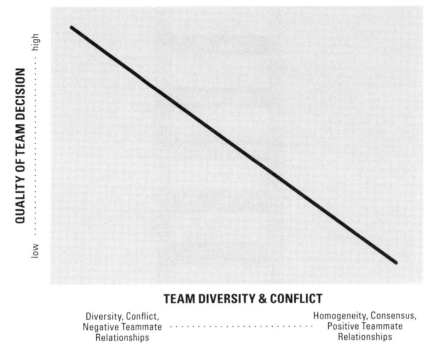

Figure 6.1. Decision quality conflict paradox. Better decisions result when diverse group members use their diverse perspectives to question one another and synergize their experiences, but the diversity and questioning can create tensions that make it difficult for teams to function in the long term.

respect that questions and disagreements are not delivered or intended as threats to identity—easier said than done. Some tools for doing so are discussed later in the chapter.

Clarify Conflict

People might not know why they disagree with each other, or they may talk past each other because they are unclear where the disagreement lies. The "ladder of inference" provides a tool to clarify where differences actually occur so mediation can focus there (Figure 6.2). Wicked situations are composed of multiple dimensions—metaphorical rungs

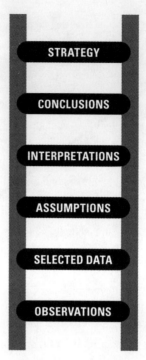

Figure 6.2. Ladder of inference. Identifying where disagreement exists so people are not frustrated by talking past one another. (Adapted from Chris Argyris, *Reasoning, Learning, and Action: Individual and Organizational* [San Francisco: Jossey-Bass, 1982].)

of a ladder. Different understandings of a wicked situation can emerge at any rung. At the base of the ladder are data, facts, and observations, and debate can focus on which data are more trustworthy, reliable, or relevant than others. Further up the ladder, the debate can focus on interpretations, causes, and implications for action. Let's illustrate with another climate change example. Everyone may agree that the amount of carbon dioxide in the atmosphere is now above 400 parts per million. People may differ on assumptions about what caused the increased atmospheric carbon. They may also differ on the conclusions they reach about whether the impacts will be disruptive. Even more differences emerge at the highest levels of inference when deciding what actions should be taken. For example, should we do nothing about climate change, impose government regulations to cap carbon emissions, invent carbon-free fuels, build sea walls to protect cities, geo-engineer the climate? Explicitly using the ladder of inference to unpack a situation improves decision making because it helps focus attention on where differences exist. It is also an effective way to ensure that the group is discussing the same problem before moving on to any proposed solutions or actions.

Frame the Facts

Facts do not exist independently of context. Mental frames provide the context people use to interpret facts. So when you present a fact, you also need to provide the frame, or else you lose control over how the fact is understood. Think of a frame as a collection of ideas literally woven together in our neural networks. George Lakoff, a leading cognitive scientist and master framer, explains it as follows:[8]

> All of our knowledge makes use of frames, and every word is defined through the frames it neurally activates. All thinking and talking involves "framing." . . . In short, one cannot avoid framing. The only question is, whose frames are being activated and hence strengthened in the brains of [listeners]. . . . And, of course, negating a frame just activates the frame, as when Nixon said, "I am not a crook" and everyone thought of him as a crook. When President Obama said that he had no intention of a "government takeover," he was activating the government-takeover frame. . . . Always go on offense, never defense. Never accept the [opponent's] frames, don't negate them, or repeat them, or structure your arguments to counter them. That just activates their frames in the brain.

When you know people are using the same frame to interpret a fact, such as when you are in their filter bubble, share their worldview, and are preaching to the choir, then you don't have to think much about framing your facts. But when people exist in nonoverlapping filter bubbles, then managing the frames by which people make sense of facts can be as important as the facts themselves.

Some frames trigger identity protective reasoning likely to polarize stakeholders into camps that will interpret facts differently. Try instead to trigger unifying frames that most people share and care about. For example, when presenting facts about water risks, frame the facts as promoting family health and national security instead of framing them as enforcing the Clean Water Act or heeding the warnings of experts working from the United Nations. The latter framing may encourage the facts to be interpreted by some stakeholders as an example of government overreach by misguided elites, when instead you want the fact to be a reason to mobilize citizen action that promotes public safety. Sustainability debates are full of these triggers. Table 6.2 summarizes a few.

The breakthrough framing presented in the first section of this book provides an example. It contrasts with a declinist framing that connects

Table 6.2. Framing Sustainability

Polarizing frames	Unifying frames
Government regulation	Health
Taxes and welfare	Family
Religion, faith, God	Freedom
Globalism versus localism	Fairness
Urban versus rural	Security
Immigration	Trustworthiness
United Nations	Responsibility
Experts, science, elites	Prosperity
Animal versus human rights	Equal opportunity
Power and privilege	Rule of law
Biodiversity versus jobs	Dignity of employment

the same facts but emphasizes overpopulation, resource exhaustion, inequity, and poverty. The declinist framing suggests things are bad and will soon get worse. Declinism triggers fear as a motivator for action. It suggests ecological and social collapse is under way and that society must change, but it does not offer a clear direction for that change, other than reversing course.

The breakthrough framing connects the same facts in a way that provides a hopeful and optimistic interpretation of current conditions. Yes, we must navigate a bottleneck of wicked challenges, any one of which can collapse civilization. Yes, sacrifices are needed, and business as usual must change. But if we do so, then we can break through to prosperity, health, and biodiversity.

The declinist and breakthrough frames connect many of the same facts and anecdotes about the world, but they suggest very different futures and encourage us to play very different roles. Which framing do you recommend?

Use Images and Graphics

Present your information visually. For example, people are more likely to accept that climate change is happening when presented with simple graphs showing increasing temperature rather than explaining the same trend with text.[9] Text requires extra mental effort to process. And, of course, you are familiar with the adage "a picture is worth a thousand words."

While the suggestion is simple, the practice is difficult. Good graphics and images are hard to create. Consultancies such as Water Words That Work provide workshops and assistance.

Manage Identity

Direction, alignment, and commitment may be better promoted by focusing on identity rather than facts. Here we discuss several strategies:

- Trigger group identity.
- Affirm self-worth.
- Play nice.
- Yes, and.
- Minimize identity conflict.
- Complicate the story.
- Find a new story.

Trigger Group Identity

You can promote direction, alignment, and commitment by triggering group identity. When people join or feel they belong to a group, they adopt and commit to that group's facts and logic. Therefore, if you want people to share and promote sustainability, then get them to identify with a group that supports or defends sustainability.

The third section of this book contains a specific example of this strategy. Menus of Change is an effort that uses group identity to get people to eat less meat and thus practice more sustainable diets. They do so by recruiting celebrity chefs to adopt and advocate recipes and menus that use less meat. Foodies and aspiring chefs desire to be like the celebrities—to be in the in-group. As a result of joining, they not only change their own diets, recipes, and menus, they also become advocates for eating less meat. That is, they not only change their own behaviors, they become influencers advocating behavior change in others—creating a ripple effect of changed menus, recipes, diets, and tastes that has helped to dramatically reduce meat eating, which is perhaps one of the most significant advances toward sustainability in recent years.

You can also trigger group identity to promote collaboration. Recall from the discussion of identity protective reasoning that people are social creatures who want to belong to and be respected by others in their group. Collaboration, therefore, will be more likely if collaborators develop and share an identity rather than identify with groups that differentiate and divide them. For example, consider a single large organization where silos exist that distinguish legal, engineering, administration, accounting, and production departments, each with its own culture and structure. If you take a few individuals from each siloed department and ask them to collaboratively plan an organization-wide effort, you risk that they will defend the positions, facts, and identities of the silos they represent. But if you get them to see themselves as members of a new, innovative, respected group, then they will be more likely to identify with that new group and thus be more open to collaboration.

Boundary Spanning Leadership, a successful approach for promoting collaborating across differences, refers to this process as "suspending boundaries," "reframing boundaries," and "developing community."[10] It occurs when people step outside their preexisting identities (whether that be a siloed department, demographic group, political affiliation, or geographic location), step inside a new group identity, and form relationships unbounded by constraints of old group memberships. One tactic promoting this outcome is to focus on values, mission, and purpose that people share, rather than attributes that differentiate them. Another tactic is to use neutral locations, such as local cafes, "creativity labs," and "serendipity areas" so that no stakeholder is reminded of turf they have to defend. Another tactic is to promote the identity of the new group by giving it a name and brand and by distributing swag such as hats and shirts with logos, coordinating colors, or mottoes.

Affirm Self-Worth

Make people feel good about themselves, confident in who they are and what they bring to the collaboration. Doing so makes them less defensive, less likely to invoke identity protective reasoning, more curious, and more likely to think carefully about an argument's facts and logic.[11]

Short exercises conducted at the beginning of a stakeholder meeting—variations of common icebreakers—can affirm self-worth. For example, a facilitator might ask participants to share something they are proud of with the group. Or participants might be asked to think about a value that is important to them—such as family or honesty—and share a story about a time they lived up to that value. Private affirmation works as well; for example, get participants to jot down three positive traits and think of examples where they lived up to those positive traits.

The affirmation exercise should happen before discussing controversial topics. Less obviously, the affirmation exercise should focus on the whole person. If the affirmation focuses specifically on the topic being debated, then people may become more entrenched and more defensive because the exercise pumped up their identification with that issue. For example, prior to a stakeholder meeting to create sustainability standards for a supply chain, don't use an exercise that reminds people of their business expertise and experience. Instead, have people think about their past civic contributions and dedication to their neighbors. Make them feel good about being a citizen rather than feeling good about being a market competitor.

Affirmation techniques work one-on-one, as well. As you banter with people, make them feel appreciated and good about themselves: pay them a compliment, recount some past accomplishment, or show appreciation for their contributions. These standard best practices of making friends and influencing people work, in part, because they bolster identity and make the person more receptive to new information and more likely to align their elephant with yours.

Play Nice

To state the obvious: don't attack someone's identity. Ad hominem attacks are not productive. Instead, get other elephants to like your elephant; then they will be more receptive to you, your perspective, and your ideas. Buy them a coffee. Find something you both enjoy. If their elephants like you and think you share some aspect of humanity with them, then they may lean your way and agree with you even before their rider hears your arguments. Being nice is another way of practicing the familiar and proven negotiation tactic of being easy on the person but hard on the problem. Don't focus your critique on the person by questioning their competency or affiliations; they will see you as an enemy and engage identity protective reasoning.

Yes, And

Avoid saying "but." When you respond to someone's comments with "but," you imply they are wrong and that you are going to tell them the truth, which provokes defensiveness and identity protective reasoning. Instead say "yes," which implies you respect their ideas. By following the "yes" with "and" you can offer alternative facts, logic, and framing that you think are important. "Yes, and" invites someone to engage your argument rather than defend their identity. It continues the conversation. The "yes, and" tool has a long and distinguished history in theater and comedy improvisation as a method to keep the dialogue and interaction going.

Minimize Identity Conflict

First, let's distinguish between identity conflict (sometimes called affective conflict) and cognitive conflict. Cognitive conflict emerges when people use different facts, logic, perspectives, and assumptions. As noted earlier in the chapter, cognitive conflict can be productive, if properly managed, because better decisions result when people question assumptions and bring different perspectives. Identity conflict emerges when someone feels their identity is threatened or disrespected. Identity conflict most always degrades group deliberations because it invokes identity protective reasoning. It poisons collaborative efforts and needs to be avoided.

Perhaps the biggest challenge to minimizing identity conflict is managing ourselves. When someone criticizes your ideas, it often feels like they are attacking you personally, trying to make you look bad, under-mining your budget, or grabbing for power. As a result, you invoke identity protective reasoning, ignore the facts, and launch into defense mode. Collaborators need to be coached to recognize that everyone has a tendency to misinterpret criticisms of their ideas as criticisms of their identities.

Tools to manage identity conflict are similar to those discussed else-where in this chapter, such as active listening, empathy, and being nice to others but hard on problems. These and other strategies are summa-rized in Table 6.3 and discussed next.[12]

Table 6.3. Responses to Identity Conflict

	Constructive	Destructive
Passive	Delay responding Cool down Reflective thinking	Avoiding Yielding Hiding emotions Self-criticizing
Active	Perspective taking Active listening Expressing emotions Reaching out Reframing	Winning at all costs Displaying anger Demeaning others Retaliating

Create the expectation that conflict can be productive and will need to be managed. Sustainable development is intensely political. We must expect that buttons will be pushed, differences in values uncovered, and identities threatened. Carefully frame critiques so they target ideas, not identities. Be prepared to step back, or help others step back, before making a response to a critique. Create an opportunity to cool down, get perspective, and reflect on what triggered the feelings of being threatened. Try to find time for emotional calm and reason to prevail, and refocus the discussion on helpful, cognitive conflict.

Even if you slow down enough to cool down, you will eventually need to mitigate the perceived conflict, which means you will need to engage someone or some topic that initially triggered the identity conflict. You might as well be the one who leads by example, reaches out, and reengages. Swallow hard and accept the discomfort. If the conflict can be reframed as a cognitive conflict rather than an identity conflict, then the opportunity emerges for using the new understandings to create space for a novel solution. Use your empathy. Try to see the situation from the other person's perspective—walk in their shoes—to identify possible reasons why the person did what they did (reasons other than to push your hot button). Try active listening to better understand how and why the other side sees the conflict. Just the act of listening can lessen the tension because it evidences that you care about the people and the problem. At the appropriate time, consider sharing your interpretations of the situation. Disclosing your feelings can be a powerful way to generate affinity trust, a key component of collaboration, discussed later in the chapter.

Complicate the Story

We discuss the power of story multiple times in this book because stories help people make sense of the world, connect the dots, understand cause and motive, and anticipate roles they and others can play in shaping the future. Understanding how to use stories, therefore, is a powerful leadership capacity. In chapter 5 we introduced the use of stories as a leadership concept and explained how stories help connect and coordinate the behaviors of dispersed stakeholders who never meet. Chapter 7 explains how stories help make sense of uncertain situations.

This section explains how stories can become problematic and hinder collaboration when they are oversimplified. Unfortunately, most of us tend to oversimplify stories, especially by stereotyping the actors and looking for quick solutions, when we encounter stressful conflict, such as negotiating a wicked sustainability challenge. We do this because stress narrows our field of attention, we become defensive about threats to our identity, and we focus on identifying others who are the source of that threat. That is, at moments of conflict, when ways to promote collaboration are most needed, the human tendency to simplify stories makes collaboration more difficult.

Oversimplified stories replace uniqueness and nuance with generalizations. For example, individual stakeholders get lumped into categories: us, them, friend, enemy, other, rural, urban, elite, immigrant, denier, Republican, Democrat. Accurate, specific details about stakeholders get ignored in favor of a few broad stereotypes that define people only as members of a group or category. Stakeholders, which were once seen as distinct individuals representing a diversity of values and positions, now seem monolithic and homogeneous despite their diversity and divisions. Instead of trying to understand what makes each stakeholder tick, simplified stories focus energies on critiquing "them" and questioning "their" motives. None of this bodes well for collaboration.

Thus a useful leadership practice is to try to complicate the story.[13] Attend to details that add complexity to the situation and the people involved. Emphasize details that don't fit the story, identify contradictions, and don't try to make all parts of the argument consistent. Remind stakeholders that life is rarely as coherent or simple as we'd like. Every person is unique and every issue has more than two sides. Ask questions that solicit details: What is oversimplified about this issue? How is your life impacted? What do you think the other side wants? What do you need to learn about them?

Find a New Story

What do the American Revolution, the avalanche of environmental legislation in the 1960s and '70s, civil rights, the Arab Spring, gay marriage, and #metoo have in common? A new story! Cass Sunstein, in *How Change Happens*, explains that something all successful social movements share is the emergence of a new story that frees people to say something new, to explain what they actually want and expect, and to cast a fresh light on the past. New stories convert what was a sense of embarrassment, and possibly shame, into a sense of dignity. They create new meanings and interpretations of events. They reconnect the dots so as to provide an alternative justification of facts, relationships, and outcomes. Stories create new identities.

A new story can be pivotal in multistakeholder collaborative efforts.[14] A story can emerge that saves face, creates new alliances, and provides breakthroughs. The power of these moments can be so profound that participants report remembering exactly when they emerged. Tactics that encourage new stories include stepping back from the specifics to see the larger system, entertaining novel solutions, deepening relationships among stakeholders, and most of all, being alert. It is difficult to predict or impose a new story from outside because, in wicked situations, stakeholders must co-construct the problem and the solution; thus new stories typically emerge from stakeholders. By being alert to their presence and power, you can allow, nurture, and celebrate new stories.

Navigate Differences

Just to repeat the obvious: stakeholders have different values, agendas, identities, and understandings of a situation. Collaboration requires overcoming some of these differences. Here we summarize tactics adapted from established collaboration toolkits.[15] The order in which they are presented is intentional: you need to do the latter, but you must first accomplish the former.

- Develop self-awareness.
- Learn how to explain yourself.
- Respect differences.

- Use active listening and empathy.
- Express interests not positions.

Develop Self-Awareness

You must be aware of what motivates you. What are your values and biases? The better you know the tendencies of your elephant, the better you can mitigate the triggers that predispose you to react negatively or positively to potential collaborators. And, of course, you need to know yourself before you can know others.

Becoming self-aware can be uncomfortable. It requires introspection and feedback most of us would rather avoid. Most leadership training programs administer batteries of diagnostics that help clients learn about their personality (e.g., introverted or extroverted), influence style (e.g., rational or inspiring), conflict style (e.g., avoider or collaborator), and so on. Websites such as YourMorals.org and SustainabilityValues.com offer free assessment tools.

Importantly, once you've been provided the results of an assessment, don't use it as an excuse. For example, even if a diagnostic classifies you as an extreme introvert, you sometimes need to act extroverted, and even if your conflict type is avoider, situations sometimes require that you engage and collaborate. Leadership often requires you to work against type and contribute what the situation demands.

Learn How to Explain Yourself

Many of us lack the language, logic, and confidence to explain our values, assumptions, and personality types to people who differ from us. We need practice. But most of us feel vulnerable sharing intimate information, so it is often easiest to practice with people similar to us—perhaps with people of the same organization, neighborhood, demographic, political party, or profession. Sharing and listening helps us become more aware of our own values, identities, and positions, as well as refine a language to explain those characteristics.

Respect Differences

Once you recognize your own characteristics and are comfortable explaining them, then you need to recognize and accept that people differ from you in how they understand and interpret the world. This is no easy task. You must avoid the tendency of your elephant to quickly evaluate and dismiss others. Values and identities that are different than yours are not wrong, they are just different. Pluralism, a bedrock of collaboration, requires recognizing and tolerating differences.

Use Active Listening and Empathy

Now for the hard part! Listen for the merits in someone's arguments. Try to understand their values and assumptions. People need to know they've been heard. If it's not clear they've been understood, then they may become defensive, which can trigger identity protective reasoning. Ask questions that draw them out and create safe spaces for them to explain their positions and values. Suspend judgment and instead strive for clarification. "Why" may be your most important question. In other words, to disagree well, you must first understand well. If someone feels confident that you've listened to them, they may listen to you.

Misinterpreting others is common. One way to know if you understand someone is to restate what you think you heard, letting the other person know you've heard and digested their point and giving them a chance to clarify. It is not sufficient to just say, "I understand." Instead, say, "I understand [your point of view] and why it makes you feel [an emotion], and I appreciate [your reasoning or beliefs]." Consider the example of a climate activist searching for merit in the arguments of a coal mining advocate.[16]

The climate activist probably won't find value in the stance that mining coal should continue. But she might be able to see merit in the reasons and beliefs underlying that stance. She might say: I understand that you believe coal mining supports your economy and culture (i.e., demonstrating understanding) and that efforts to close the mine make you angry (i.e., appreciating emotion) because it threatens your family and your heritage. Therefore, I can see the value in you wanting to continue mining even if doing so contributes to eventual climate change (i.e., showing that she sees merit in the other person's reasoning).

"Empathy is the antidote to righteousness." So argues Jonathan Haight in *Righteous Mind*. If you want someone to collaborate with you, you'll need to see things from their perspective, and you'll want them to do the same for you. You need to grant others moral respect by being sympathetic to their motives and reasoning. You need to find ways to walk in their shoes, see the situation from their perspective. You need to actively listen and be open to being persuaded by what they say. Strategies for facilitating active listening and empathy include the following:

Peacekeeping circles: Use this strategy adapted from aborginal cultures. Arranging stakeholders in a circle breaks down the hierarchy. A talking piece is passed and only the one holding it speaks. A facilitator maintains order. Decisions are not made. The goal of coming together is not to change others but to be understood and to understand.

Interviews: Prepare a series of open-ended questions that explore the situation and a person's role in it. What does the issue mean to them? How did they get involved? Why? What is a good outcome for their organization or community? What likely or potential outcomes concern them? Why? The goal is to make the person feel thoroughly heard.

Shadowing: Follow beside someone as they deal with the situation and issues being debated. What is their day-to-day life like? What do they do, and what decisions do they make? Reflect on how you would do the same.

Learning journeys: Leave the familiar behind and go to see the situation firsthand. It can be as simple as visiting another part of your community, or as involved as traveling to another country to explore your supply chain.

Express Interests Not Positions

The widely applied and proven strategy known as Interest-Based Negotiation[17] builds on this simple principle: Start by explaining your interests. Ask: Why do you care? This presents an invitation to collaborate. It allows you to ask: What do you care about? If you start, instead, by stating a position, then you leave less room to negotiate. Confronted with a position, other stakeholders tend to dig in their heels and offer counterpositions: You want ABC? We don't. We want XYZ! The elephants very quickly lean one way or the other, and empathy, openness to change, and collaboration become more difficult.

For example, rather than a stakeholder insisting they want "cap and trade" as a solution to climate change, they can instead say they are interested in protecting future jobs, family health, and species diversity endangered by climate change. This request leaves open the space for potential collaborators to say they too want jobs plus national security. These stakeholders could then explore innovative policies such as a revenue-neutral, border-adjusted, carbon-fee-and-dividend policy that keeps revenue within a country, sustains local jobs, promotes national security, and reduces emissions. By focusing first on interests, they can then explore positions that satisfy those interests.

Build and Repair Trust

Collaborating across differences is impossible without trust. Trust allows stakeholders to be vulnerable and open to change, to listen to one another, to believe that promises made will be promises kept, and thus to be willing to risk the time and reputation that collaborative efforts require. Distrust makes stakeholders wary of collaboration: they expect lies, disrespect, lack of commitment, and even a disingenuous use of the process.

Trust has four dimensions: dispositional, rational, affinitive, and process.[18] Table 6.4 defines each type and discusses the implications for promoting and repairing trust. In chapter 14, a case study of the Fire Learning Network illustrates how trust enables collaboration.

Collaboration is likely to be resilient and effective over the long term if all four types of trust are maintained. If something damages one type of trust, other forms may serve as a buffer until the lost trust is rebuilt. For example, if a charismatic stakeholder that everyone likes leaves the group, then the group loses some of its affinity trust. The collaboration is more likely to survive if the group has strong rational and process trust; which is more likely to exist if other stakeholders have been competent and respectful of one another and abide by effective, jointly decided procedures to make and enforce decisions. Likewise, if one stakeholder fails to deliver and rational trust is lost, collaboration is more likely to continue if sanctions outlined in the procedures are enforced—that is, if the process is trusted and functions as expected. If one or more of the trust dimensions is low or damaged, then anyone in the group can practice leadership by facilitating activities, such as those already discussed, that restore trust.

Trust in the process is especially important at the beginning of a collaborative effort, when people don't have enough experience to like or rationally trust other stakeholders, or might have reasons from past encounters not to trust them. Joining a new collaborative effort risks wasting time and damaging one's reputation. Stakeholders need to be convinced that their views will be heard, that criticism will be constructive, that the process will be fair, and that other stakeholders will stay committed through the time it takes to achieve direction, alignment,

Table 6.4. Managing Trust

Type	Definition	How to promote
Dispositional	Innate tendency: some people are more trusting than others.	Difficult to change.
Rational	Based on perceptions of competence, predictability, and past performance. If someone proved themselves trustworthy in the past—if they delivered on promises and treated others with respect—then it is rational to expect them to do so again.	Hold people accountable. If someone fails to deliver on promises or is disrespectful, then implement procedures to hold them accountable until they prove it is rational to trust them again.
Affinitive	Feelings of social connectedness, positive shared experiences, shared identities, group membership, and being liked.	Promoted by naming the group, distributing hats or shirts with logos, celebrating group milestones, and rewarding individual contributions to the group with certificates, awards, or pats on the back. Also use standard best practices of being respectful, using active listening, and attempting empathy.
Process	Confidence that the process is fair and that compliance and best practices will be enforced.	Procedures and rules are developed by participants, transparent, and consistently applied; particularly anything regarding group membership and decision making.

and commitment. An external actor with legitimacy and resources can help create enough trust in the system for the collaboration to begin, creating what is called a holding space.[19]

Holding spaces are more than locations; they are combinations of reputation, place, and process that use preexisting relationships and the status of the convener to bring people to the table and to hold everyone accountable. Holding spaces minimize distractions and tangents by focusing attention to the problems, issues, or controversies that need to be resolved, and on the opportunities for collaboration. Holding spaces frame issues, presenting them as constructive solutions worth considering rather than threats to be avoided. Holding spaces also provide a safe forum for conflicting perspectives to be voiced, recognized, and respected, rather than ignored and suppressed.

Form Partnerships

A formal partnership between organizations offers a very specific type of collaboration with detailed expectations for shared responsibility. The detail and formality become necessary because partners become vulnerable to each other's failure and misbehavior. This section reviews attributes of these formal partnerships that emphasize the need to work across differences. Chapter 15 of this book presents a case study about a public–private partnership using green infrastructure to solve a community's stormwater management challenges.

Partnering requires recognizing and managing differences between partnering organizations: not just orchestrating the different strengths needed to solve the problem, but managing differences in how organizations operate, including different internal cultures, decision-making styles, communication strategies, outcome reporting, and reward structures. Great resources exist that explain best practices of successful partnerships.[20] Many of these practices are summarized in Table 6.5 and reflect tools addressed elsewhere in this and prior chapters.

Partnering is related to collective impact, a strategy discussed in chapter 5. Collective impact coordinates many actors distributed across a

Table 6.5. Partnering Best Practices

Best practices	Description
Establish shared goals and mutual benefit	Clear, honest, robust discussion is needed to shape, share, and understand the partnership's goals. To be sustainable, the partnership must provide specific benefits to each partner.
Respect partner strengths and weaknesses	Partners contribute different skills, resources, experience, and authority. A business partner, for example, has skills managing supply chains and labor, while a government partner has the power to convene. They also face different risks to reputation, autonomy, and resources.
Explicit governance mechanisms	Appropriate and efficient governance helps avoid misunderstandings and conflict by defining roles, expectations, and means of resolving conflict. It should be renegotiable.
Accountability	Evaluate activities using mutually agreed-upon standards. Accept responsibility for one's actions. Be responsive to sanctions from partners for those actions.
Transparency	Evaluations should be accurate, timely, accessible, and trusted.
Fill key roles	At different stages of the partnership, different roles become critical, including champions, brokers, managers, and external advocates.
Create a learning culture	Share and learn from successes and mistakes.
Manage trust	Establishing shared goals promotes rational trust. Respecting strengths and weaknesses develops affinity, rational trust, and system trust. Clear governance, accountability, and transparency establishes process trust. A learning culture builds both rational and system trust.

vast system to simultaneously influence a large set of interconnected outcomes. That collective effort will likely involve formal partnerships where organizations coordinate their efforts to address some aspect of the larger project. Partnerships tend to be more specific in focus and involve fewer stakeholders.

Conclusion

Given the scope and scale of wicked Anthropocene challenges, the need has never been greater for collaboration among multiple, diverse stakeholders. Nor has collaboration been more difficult: we are divided and diverging because of confirmation bias, identity protective reasoning, filter bubbles, echo chambers, and network propaganda loops. Overcoming these challenges requires perseverance and integrity, as well as a leadership toolbox filled with strategies such as those reviewed here; sadly, even that may not be enough in some situations.

CHAPTER 7

Adapting to Change, Uncertainty, and Failure

The Anthropocene requires practices for promoting direction, alignment, and commitment in novel situations characterized by confounding uncertainty and dynamism. This chapter introduces several practices and principles that facilitate adaptive leadership.

- Sensemaking
- Learning by doing
- Innovating
- Being disruptive
- Striving for resiliency
- Anticipating the future with scenario planning
- Sharing lessons
- Sensemaking

The confounding uncertainty of the Anthropocene complicates decision making. Consider the following conundrum.

Like most professionals, you are wary of offering advice when likely to be wrong and blamed for failure. So you err on the side of caution and pause to collect additional information in the search for clarity and certainty. But wicked situations are complex, dynamic, and unique, so additional information is unlikely to help, and you get stuck in analysis-paralysis. That means you've delayed the decision, which means you've allowed the status quo to continue, which means you've probably enabled worse outcomes than if you had acted and failed. Moreover, by not acting, you missed the opportunity to learn how the system responds to interventions: one of the key tenets of learning by doing, and probably what you should be doing if you want to make sense of a wicked situation. But you know that if you rush into a decision, you may misinterpret it, because you've seen research showing that experts actually don't do well in ambiguous and uncertain situations: experts tend to fall victim to confirmation bias that selectively identifies observations that fit their theories and past experiences. You've also been told that people make poor decisions about unique situations when they are stressed, hurried, and have limited information. In such situations, most people instead invoke stereotypes, see patterns where none exist, and subconsciously paper over anomalies. And, most importantly, you are aware of the sunk-cost fallacy: once a decision gets made, people tend to defend and repeat the same or similar decision, regardless of whether it is working, because to stop and try something different is to suggest that the time, resources, and people who supported the efforts were wasted. So, knowing all this, you are cautious to make quick decisions, which brings you back to analysis-paralysis and supporting the status quo, which you know is bad, so what should you do?[1]

If you find yourself in such situations, then sensemaking provides a way forward. Sensemaking has two aspects: mindset and practice.

Sensemaking as *mindset* requires being flexible and taking enough time to consult others and broaden your perspective, but not so much time that you get trapped in analysis-paralysis. When things are highly uncertain, better decisions emerge when ideas are proposed, tested, rejected, and replaced with new ideas to retest, again and again and again. That means you must be courageous enough to propose and make decisions, while being humble enough to abandon what does not work, following the sensemaking principle of strong ideas weakly held. A sensemaking mindset encourages course corrections rather than rigidly following a planned path toward a predetermined solution. It promotes tolerance for results that differ from those that were predicted.

Sensemaking as a *practice* is the focus of the remainder of this section. Many sensemaking practices exist.[2] The 3SO SenseMaking Tool, outlined here, is based on a simple and obvious axiom: stakeholders use strategies to influence system outcomes (Figure 7.1). It helps you unpack four dimensions present in most every sustainability situation: stakeholders, strategies, systems, and outcomes. To make sense of a situation, you should work iteratively through each of these four dimensions. What you learn from one dimension (i.e., stakeholders) can inform and help you more effectively see relevant information in another dimension (i.e., the strategies stakeholders use, or the outcomes they want).

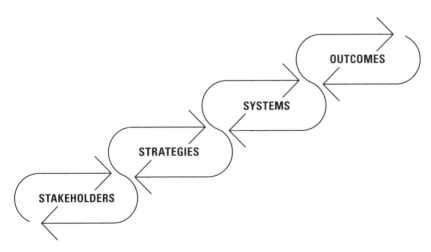

Figure 7.1. 3SO sensemaking practice. A process for asking questions and engaging a wicked problem to avoid analysis-paralysis in the face of confounding uncertainty.

Chapter 12 of this book illustrates this sensemaking approach using a story about carbon farming as an innovative and hopeful strategy for addressing climate change.

Next we describe each of the four dimensions of the 3SO SenseMaking Tool and sources of uncertainty that must be navigated.

Stakeholders

Begin with a stakeholder analysis.[3] Stakeholders are actors (e.g., individuals, organizations) that have an interest or influence relevant to the situation. Who are they, and what do they care about? Some stakeholders might be actively shaping the outcomes, others might be trying to get involved but are being ignored, and some will be oblivious of the situation but need to be engaged if meaningful change is to result. A simple analysis of stakeholder interest and influence helps differentiate "material" stakeholders, who need to be fully engaged, from those that just need to be informed or ignored (Table 7.1). Stakeholders with low interest and little influence require limited attention. In contrast, stakeholders with much to win or lose, and who can bring considerable resources to advance or stall progress, require active engagement.

A challenge in identifying relevant stakeholders is that Anthropocene challenges are dispersed over space and time (Table 7.2). As an example, take a community trying to map and manage water risks. The

Table 7.1. Stakeholder Materiality Matrix

	Low interest	High interest
High influence	Keep satisfied Seek consent Avoid veto power	Fully engage Build consensus
Low influence	Monitor Ignore	Keep informed Solicit feedback Seek consent

Table 7.2. Stakeholders with Impacts

Impact	Type of stakeholder
Upstream	Stakeholders involved with the infrastructure, raw materials, and basic services upon which the product or event depend (e.g., electricity, roads, media, education)
Direct	Stakeholders engaged in producing the product and its packaging, participating in the event, or supplying the things that make the event or product happen
Downstream and use	Stakeholders involved in servicing, using, storing, distributing, cleaning, and the resources and services needed to support those functions (e.g., refrigeration)
Enabled impacts	Stakeholder behaviors and other impacts that change as the result of the product or event; perhaps creating substitutes, or efficiencies, or consumption patterns that change overall impact

direct stakeholders are those associated with water used and rain falling within the political boundaries of the community. But *upstream* stakeholders might be even more important. The obvious upstream stakeholders include the users and polluters of water sources that flow into the local water supply. The less obvious upstream stakeholders include those that impact goods and services upon which the community depends. For example, the production of food and electricity requires enormous amounts of water, and thus communities are dependent on and responsible for the water used wherever their food and electricity are produced. Even more consequential and less obvious are stakeholders associated with *enabled* impacts. A business might be responsible for strategies or technologies that help others manage their water risks or reduce their carbon footprint, thereby benefiting stakeholders with no visible connection other than their adoption of and dependence on these strategies and technologies. Information technology companies that support "smart cities" or "precision agriculture" provide examples. With improved monitoring, cities can manage traffic flows in ways that reduce greenhouse gas emissions, and farms can improve soil health and crop productivity while reducing inputs of water, fertilizer, and biocides.[4]

Stakeholders introduce a huge amount of uncertainty into most situations because they don't always know what they want, can be fickle, and, if identity is threatened, can be volatile. For example, many sustainability situations produce winners and losers—somebody's history gets preserved and celebrated, but another's dreams of development get dashed; an ecosystem that provided services gets paved over to meet the housing needs of a community; a species gets saved from extinction but jobs are lost, and so on. Consider coal mining—if your ancestors and family members found employment in the production, transportation, finance, or support services of coal, then the decline of the coal industry not only hurts your paycheck it challenges your identity. When someone argues that coal mining needs to end, they question your heritage and diminish the contribution of your family to society. In such identity conflicts, it is impossible to predict who will compromise, who will fold, and who will persist to the bitter end. The winners might be those with power, status, and access to media, or the winners might be those with the most conviction and the strongest narratives.

Strategies

Strategies are the things stakeholders do to capture opportunities, overcome challenges, and change systems. Strategies are the interventions, treatments, projects, policies, and efforts that stakeholders organize and implement. Strategies are informed by theories of change and are an attempt to tinker with system functions. Key tasks of sensemaking are identifying the strategies stakeholders use, understanding how these strategies are expected to work and what system outcomes they are meant to produce, and being intentional about assessing their successes and failures.

Types of strategies include governance and regulation, market fixes, finance and investment, technological innovation, and changing consumer and voter behavior:

- Governance and regulation include limits and fines for pollution, product testing and approval, land-use planning, building codes, minimum standards, best practices, and labor rights.
- Market fixes include attempts to internalize externalities with tax incentives, polluter pay fees, cap and trade policies, price ecosystem services, and carbon taxes, as well as social entrepreneurship that creates new business models.
- Property rights fixes include easements, zoning, public ownership, purchasing and transfer of development rights, and privatizing the commons.
- Finance and investment strategies include divestment, shareholder action, socially responsible investment, and loans with environmental performance standards.
- Technological innovation includes increasing product energy efficiency, inventing substitute resources, direct air carbon capture, battery storage, carbon-free cement, nanotechnology, synthetic biology, green revolution agriculture, and research and development in general.
- Changing consumer and voter behavior includes advertising campaigns that influence people to shop and vote differently.

Strategies introduce another vector of uncertainty. In the changing and emerging conditions of the Anthropocene we don't know whether strategies proven to work in the past will produce the same successful results. Moreover, new challenges such as climate change will require developing new strategies of untested effectiveness. Uncertainty further increases because strategies can be as contested as political ideologies.

For example, to address the challenge of increasing and securing the food supply, should we emphasize government regulation, market innovation, pesticides, organics, genetic engineering, international collaboration, changing individual diets, or something else? Each strategy has its advocates and critics. It is difficult to predict which strategy's backers will prevail and which future they will create.

Systems

Systems thinking focuses on interrelationships and strives to examine the bigger picture where larger connective risks and opportunities may exist (i.e., seeing the forest for the trees). It promotes a broad vision of the future that extends beyond the problem at hand and exposes root causes of system failure that can be targeted for change rather than just treating symptoms. Collaborative system mapping exercises can expose assumptions and build adaptive capacity among stakeholders because they share an understanding of how the system works. Systems properties to consider mapping include the following:[5]

- The flows that course through the system, such as water, money, people, and information
- The sinks that make up the source of flows and can bring stability or vulnerability, such as water in a reservoir or cash in a bank account
- The negative feedback loops that slow change, such as species diversity that provides redundancy, protection of whistleblowers and freedom-of-information requests that promote transparency and accountability, and impact fees and performance bonds that force entrepreneurs to assume the full cost of their endeavors
- The positive feedback loops that accelerate change and lead to tipping points, such as melting Arctic ice exposing heat-absorbing waters, or the tendency of wealthy people to be able to invest in

education, technology, businesses, and networks that capture more
wealth that they then pass to heirs

- The infrastructure that connects things such as roads, electricity
  grids, and supply chains
- The rules, standards, norms, and laws that guide behavior, such as
  pollution regulations, fairness, elections, free markets, and tolerance of corruption

Systems uncertainty is increasing. Climate change, food security,
poverty reduction, and other challenges of the Anthropocene are
embedded in complex, open, unstable, and unpredictable systems of
interactions. Changes ripple through social-environmental components and trigger feedback loops, producing nonlinear change and
emergent qualities: species evolve and migrate, successful cities attract
more businesses and more talent and become more successful, cheaper
natural gas and solar energy disrupt coal economies and fuel political movements to bring back coal, improved agriculture technology
increases yields that drive down food prices and bankrupt farmers,
shared-autonomous-electric vehicles revolutionize car ownership and
transportation systems, and so on. By the end of the twentieth century,
senior members of the American Association for the Advancement of
Science acknowledged that uncertainty in coupled human–nature systems was too much for traditional science to overcome and the systems
had "radically outgrown" science's ability to explain them, let alone
predict and control them.[6] Predictions by epidemiologists about "flat-
tening the curve" of infections during the COVID-19 pandemic illustrate the uncertainty created when people are part of the system, as is
the case for most Anthropocene challenges. For some people, just providing them with information changed their behaviors. For example,
when provided information about high infection rates, many people
practiced greater social distancing, which in turn changed the infection

rate, which in turn changed behaviors, making it difficult to predict the rate of future infections.

Outcomes

Outcomes are where the proverbial rubber meets the road. They transform broad goals into specific, tangible, measurable deliverables. For example, if a goal is to mitigate climate change, a specific outcome would be to reduce greenhouse gas emissions from the transportation sector of a community by 25 percent over the next decade. A case study in chapter 11 about community energy planning provides good examples of outcome measures that made the effort successful. Some of the most powerful outcomes to identify are those used to trigger action, hold decision makers accountable, and promote learning and behavioral change.

- Trigger action: Outcome measures provide feedback that helps prioritize actions. They inform citizens, politicians, and businesses that looming problems need attention and action.
- Hold decision makers accountable: Outcome measures provide evidence of progress or backsliding and hold stakeholders accountable for progress toward goals.
- Promote learning and behavioral change: Outcome measures can connect goals and actions by showing the impacts of behaviors and showing the consequences of behavior changed.

The desired outcomes (or goals) of most collaborative efforts are contested and uncertain. This is often due to the sheer difficulty in identifying and agreeing to the problem that the collaborators hope to solve. Stakeholders often don't know what they want. Desired outcomes also change over time. For example, stakeholders may initially agree that they want to maximize wealth and freedom in their community through real estate development. After years of pursuing this goal, residents may become frustrated by the outcomes that sprawl produces: traffic congestion, fossil fuel dependence, air pollution, and the loss of local foods, open space, and biodiversity. That is, stakeholders change their goals as they experience the landscape and lifestyle those goals created. It is only after people create a future that they can decide if they want to live there. Ultimately, a stakeholder's desired outcomes can only be hypotheses about the future they hope to live in.

Learning by Doing

"Success is not final, failure is not fatal: it is the courage to continue that counts." Winston Churchill might not spring to mind as an example of a collaborative, participatory leader, but his prose captures a key challenge of wicked leadership. The confounding uncertainty of the Anthropocene will produce repeated and regular failures that require courage and continuous learning. Fortunately, the plan–do–check–fix loop offers a widely used and proven four-step approach. In the jargon of environmental professions, this process is known as adaptive management. In business, the approach is called the Deming cycle or management by discovery. In the planning profession, it is known as transactive planning, incrementalism, or groping along. Project management professionals call it the agile method. Advocates of design thinking and innovation call it piloting and pivoting. Common to all these approaches is a process that is intentional, refutable, transparent, and shareable.[7]

Learning by doing means accepting and expecting failure because success is rare and change is continuous. Whatever we do, some aspect of it usually fails, and the failure creates opportunities to learn. Reframing failure as learning empowers professionals to improve their expertise. Mathew Syed's book *Black Box Thinking: Why Most People Never Learn from Their Mistakes—But Some Do* explains how some professional cultures embrace learning from failure more than others. As an illustration, he compares aviation to medicine. Aviation has a remarkable and still-improving safety record, attributable to a culture that carefully documents and learns from mistakes—most every failure triggers an investigation using data continuously recorded by the legendary black boxes, installed just in case there is an accident. In contrast, medicine is more likely to refer to a mistake as a complication or a one-of-a-kind incident, neither of which leads to investigations that can produce lessons to be incorporated into future medical practice. As a consequence of fearing failure, Syed argues, medical mistakes have become the third leading cause of death. His reasoning and examples go further. He attributes the fruits of modernity and enlightenment to the willingness of early Greek civilization to tolerate failure and break from primitive cultures that explained every outcome—even if unwanted and unexpected—as caused by factors that can't be questioned, such as fate or gods. He also reminds us that the scientific method is powered by falsification. Making progress on the wicked challenges of the Anthropocene will require being intentional about learning by doing.

In the plan–do–check–fix approach, every "do" provides opportunities to test how the system responds to interventions, how stakeholders understand the situation, how the outcomes measure progress, how the strategies work, and so on. The plan–do–check–learn loop works best for situations that are recurrent.[8] Many such sustainability challenges exist. Agricultural and natural resource situations, for example, typically have cyclical harvest and ecological cycles, where products such as trees, ducks, fish, and switchgrass are periodically harvested, and lessons can be learned at each cycle. In manufacturing and construction, every new car or building provides lessons that improve production of the next one. In project management, teams and administrative units repeatedly work through decision-making processes that they can intentionally improve. However, many wicked situations don't repeat. They are unique and unrepeatable, which makes learning by doing more difficult.

Nonetheless, for every situation you confront, three learning opportunities are possible: single loop, double loop, and triple loop (Table 7.3). *Single-loop learning* focuses on improving understanding of system functions and strategy effectiveness—that is, did the intervention work as expected, does the product operate as expected, and can you better understand how the system functions and how the desired outcomes are produced? *Double-loop learning* focuses on the goals attempted and the questions asked. Is the problem adequately defined? Did you identify the right goals, values, and assumptions? What did stakeholders learn about themselves, one another, and the future they desire? *Triple-loop learning* involves learning how to learn. It requires reflecting on whether you took enough time and effort to learn from what was done, and building capacity in people that will likely do something similar in the future.

Table 7.3. Lessons from Learning by Doing/Failing

Single-loop learning	Improve how strategies change systems by monitoring outcomes. Failure results from using the wrong strategy, or a strategy that needs improvement. Learning improves our models, theories, and predictions about the world.
Double-loop learning	Question and improve goals, assumptions, and worldviews about how we decide what we want and what is right. Failure results from asking the wrong questions and not agreeing on what defines success. Learning helps set feasible goals and define a future where we want to live.
Triple-loop learning	Improve how we learn by being intentional about using a process that helps us learn and makes the process more trusted, intentional, refutable, transparent, and shared.

An all too common obstacle to learning is inadequate commitment to evaluation. It is easy to generate excitement and commitment at the beginning of an intervention—people bask in the spotlight of ribbon-cutting ceremonies that accompany efforts to solve problems—but collecting good information about why the effort failed is less glamorous and less well funded. Stakeholders must commit the resources needed to assess outcomes so lessons can be extracted. Therefore, leadership will be needed to sustain direction, alignment, and commitment to the plan–do–check–fix approach. Sunset provisions that terminate a program or periodically require reauthorization, for example, force evaluation and help mitigate the tendency of programs to become institutionalized. Framing new initiatives as experimental may also help. Doing so puts in place the expectation that the policy or program is temporary, likely to fail, in need of evaluation, and expected to be replaced.

Innovating

Technological innovation, social innovation, and entrepreneurship are a suite of strategies intended to address wicked challenges by disrupting the status quo. These strategies bring together stakeholders with diverse expertise, experience, and resources to reimagine a situation and a solution. Innovation may be necessary and useful when business-as-usual produces bad outcomes and missed opportunities, but strategies remain stuck in the past, doing the same things and rewarding the same outcomes.

The essence of innovation is captured by Thomas Edison's justification of the piloting and pivoting that led to the light bulb: "I have not failed. I just found 10,000 ways that won't work." Hopefully, enough lessons are eventually learned from each pilot and pivot to produce an innovation that has relevance, impact, and sustainability. The process of innovation requires both the problem and the solution to be reimagined. Innovators must immerse themselves in the situation, repeatedly reorienting and shifting gears until viable and practical solutions come into focus. There are many consultancies, publications, and how-to books that can provide assistance.[9] *Collaborative innovation* is a specific approach we want to highlight here because it is particularly well-suited to the wicked situations and cross-sector collaboration we emphasize in this book. Chapter 12 presents an example of carbon farming.

The collaborative innovation process is outlined in Table 7.4. It requires sufficient vision of a possible innovation to enable recruiting a core network of stakeholders with diverse and deep experience relevant to the innovation. These stakeholders in turn engage other stakeholders, with the goal of deepening their empathy and their understanding of the situation. Through carefully facilitated meetings, the core stakeholders build direction, alignment, and commitment around a specific, meaningful vision of changes that are needed. They articulate specific "critical shifts" as differences between the current state and the desired future state. These shifts provide focus and clarity about the specific changes needed to trigger something disruptive and transformative. The group brainstorms possible interventions that will trigger the disruption. Some ideas survive scrutiny and are quickly developed into testable prototypes that can be piloted with actual users to see how they work and to learn lessons from how they fail. These lessons inform revisions to the innovation, a process known as pivoting, that are in turn piloted to produce more lessons that are incorporated into subsequent pivoting and piloting. The process continues, sometimes revisiting and revising the core assumptions and goals, always piloting and pivoting. The process can be long and the outcomes uncertain, so the group must sustain the courage to completely revise their vision, goals, and strategies as they learn more and dig deeper.

Striving for Resiliency

Resiliency is a paradigm that, at its core, is concerned about unanticipated conditions that can catastrophically disrupt a system.[10] Perhaps the best way to understand resiliency is to contrast it with something more familiar: efficiency.

Table 7.4. Basic Components of Collaborative Innovation Processes

People	
Backbone organization	• Provides strategic and administrative capacity to the network • Conducts interviews to intentionally select network members • Provides administrative support to the network and initiative groups
Design team	• Consists of four to six key leaders within the network who guide the work
Network	• Representative of the entire system • High-leverage stakeholders • Change agents • Experts willing to collaborate and commit to the process
Initiative groups	• Groups within the network organized to address specific critical shifts

Process/tasks	
Identify initial, working goal	• Establish a common direction by defining specific goals and determining necessary system changes.
Conduct interviews	• Interview system leaders and stakeholders to gain insight into the system organization and the experiences of people within the system. • Use information to refine goals and identify potential members of the network.
Form network	• Invite system leaders to join the network. • Identify and select a design team.
Identify critical shifts	• Identify changes in aspects of the system that must happen if the goal is to be achieved. • Provide focus and clarity by describing how the system needs to function in the future and what it would take to create those system functions. • Generate specific actions that are exciting, energizing, and engaging, and align network efforts.
Test prototypes	• Initiative groups engage in an iterative process of prototyping, piloting, testing, soliciting feedback, and redesigning to develop effective solutions.
Deploy and scale-up solutions	• Secure resources to fully deploy and scale-up solutions.

Efficiency was the guiding paradigm of environmental management for much of the twentieth century.[11] In the name of efficiency, environmental professionals reengineered environmental systems to maximize yields of energy, water, forage, soil, trees, corn, and other resources. For example, foresters transformed forests into tree plantations to quickly produce pulp and lumber, and hydrologists transformed rivers into channels with dams to provide electric power and agricultural irrigation. The efficiency paradigm focuses stakeholder attention on minimizing inputs, maximizing outputs, and controlling system attributes to sustain continuous, predictable production.

Resiliency, in contrast, focuses attention on a system's dynamism, variability, and uncertainty. Rather than striving for the efficiency thinking goals of precision and control, resiliency thinking suggests anticipating change and emergence. Rather than design fail-safe solutions, stakeholders should design for safe failure. Resiliency thinking encourages stakeholders to look for strategies that are robust and broad, rather than efficient and specific, because such strategies are more likely to be successful under a wider range of potential future conditions. Rather than maximizing the chance of the single best outcome, resiliency seeks to maximize the likelihood of one or more acceptable and desirable outcomes.

Resiliency can be promoted by creating redundancies, stabilizing buffers, protecting negative feedback loops that slow down change, and selecting goals and directions that enhance capacity to keep options open and prevent significant harm when unanticipated changes occur. For example, prudent financial investors diversify their portfolios to protect their assets from market fluctuations and enable flexible responses to conditions that are hard to anticipate. Farmers faced with uncertain temperatures and rainfall promote resiliency by selecting crops that will grow under both wet and dry conditions. Supply chain managers promote resiliency by diversifying sourcing of vulnerable materials so that disruptions from climate change or social unrest in one location don't bring the whole production process to a grinding halt.

When viewed through the lens of efficiency, resiliency-enhancing goals come at a cost: the farmer's crops might not produce the highest yield or price, and the business with a diversified supply may pay a higher price for transportation and coordination. Is it worth it? That is the key question reflected in the tension between efficiency and resiliency. When future conditions are certain, it makes sense to strive for efficiency and to ask which actions will produce the single best outcome. But when future conditions are uncertain, it may make more sense to strive for resiliency and to ask which actions will most likely produce an outcome that doesn't disrupt those that depend on it.

Anticipating the Future with Scenario Planning

Confounding uncertainty clouds crystal balls, so what lies ahead is unknown. Yet leadership requires identifying direction, which requires anticipating that future. Scenario planning provides one tool to imagine and plan for possible futures. Scenario planning helps organizations, communities, and professionals become more nimble because they have already thought through how they might respond to possible futures. Scenario planning also provides a tool to question conventional wisdom embedded in the power structure that propels the status quo. For example, an organization could ask what would happen if the assumptions and priorities of the C-suite or agency administration were different. Scenario planning can also reveal direction and goals for leadership. If one possible future is decidedly better or worse than others, then leadership efforts can strive to create or avoid the conditions that lead to those futures.

A scenario planning process typically begins by scanning current reality to identify particularly powerful drivers of change, such as demographic trends, key policies, or technical innovations. These drivers result in outcomes that are the inevitable consequences of events that have already happened, or of trends that are already well developed. Different scenarios reflect different assumptions about those policies, innovations, and trends, and their impacts. Computer simulations, role-playing exercises, and best guesses project the implications of those futures for key outcomes that interest stakeholders.

Scenario planning originated as a military planning tool, but it became well known because Royal Dutch Shell used it to imagine what severe oil supply constraints would do to the company and to the whole oil industry. As a result of scenario planning, the corporation had contingency plans in place that helped them react more quickly and profitably to the oil shocks of 1973.

The Intergovernmental Panel on Climate Change commissioned scenarios to help anticipate the costs and implications of climate mitigation and adaptation policies. Five probable scenarios were envisioned (Table 7.5). The futures are startlingly different and illustrate why climate change presents such difficult and polarizing political decisions. As described here, the different scenarios have vastly different impacts on human population, urbanization, inequity, economic growth, energy consumed, land use, greenhouse gas emissions, and other key outcomes.

In the *fossil-fueled development* scenario, policies promote fossil fuels development and use as well as investment in education, technology, and global free trade. The resulting economic growth produces enormous wealth, widely distributed. The demographic transition, driven by prosperity and empowered women, drives human population down toward six billion, and technological innovations increase agricultural productivity enough to retire farms and increase forest and habitat for wildlife. Countries will be more wealthy and able to adapt to climate change consequences, but continued use of fossil fuels means mitigation efforts will be delayed.

Table 7.5. Possible Scenarios*

Fossil-fueled development (high challenges to mitigation, low challenges to adaptation)	This future world places increasing faith in competitive markets, innovation, and participatory societies to produce rapid technological progress and development of human capital as the path to sustainable development. Global markets are increasingly integrated. There are also strong investments in health, education, and institutions to enhance human and social capital. This push for economic and social development is coupled with the exploitation of abundant fossil fuel resources and the adoption of resource- and energy-intensive lifestyles around the world. Local environmental problems like air pollution are successfully managed. There is faith in the ability to effectively manage social and ecological systems, including by geo-engineering if necessary.
The green grow (low challenges to mitigation and adaptation)	More effective global institutions improve management of the global commons. Educational and health investments accelerate the demographic transition, and the emphasis on economic growth shifts toward a broader emphasis on human well-being. Driven by an increasing commitment to achieving sustainable development goals, inequality is reduced both across and within countries.
Business as usual (medium challenges to mitigation and adaptation)	Social, economic, and technological trends do not shift markedly from historical patterns. Development and income growth proceeds unevenly, with some countries making relatively good progress while others do not. Global and national institutions work toward but make slow progress in achieving sustainable development goals. Income inequality persists, or improves only slowly, and challenges to reducing vulnerability to societal and environmental changes remain.
Regional rivalry (high challenges to mitigation and adaptation)	A resurgent nationalism, concerns about competitiveness and security, and regional conflicts push countries to increasingly focus on domestic or, at most, regional issues. Policies shift over time toward national and

Table 7.5. continued

	regional security issues. Countries focus on achieving energy and food security goals within their own regions at the expense of broader-based development. Investments in education and technological development decline. Economic development is slow, consumption is material-intensive, and inequalities persist or worsen over time.
Inequality (low challenges to mitigation, high challenges to adaptation)	Highly unequal investments in human capital, combined with increasing disparities in economic opportunity and political power, lead to increasing inequalities and stratification both across and within countries. Over time, a gap widens between an internationally connected society that contributes to knowledge- and capital-intensive sectors of the global economy, and a fragmented collection of lower-income, poorly educated societies that work in a labor-intensive, low-tech economy. Social cohesion degrades and conflict and unrest become increasingly common. Environmental policies focus on local issues around middle- and high-income areas.

*Based on Keywan Riahi, Detlef P. Van Vuuren, Elmar Kriegler, Jae Edmonds, Brian C. O'Neill, Shinichiro Fujimori, Nico Bauer, et al. "The Shared Socioeconomic Pathways and Their Energy, Land Use, and Greenhouse Gas Emissions Implications: An Overview." *Global Environmental Change* 42 (2017): 153–168.

The *green-grow* scenario also dramatically grows the economy with investment in technology, education, and global trade, as well as global institutions that aggressively mitigate greenhouse gas emissions. People will be a bit less wealthy than in the *fossil-fueled development* scenario, so population and inequality will be higher, but mitigation is more successful, and more forest and better environmental conditions prevail.

The *rivalry* and *inequality* scenarios produce remarkably less favorable conditions. In these scenarios, investments shift toward national interests, border security, building walls, limiting global trade, and so on. There is less money to invest in developing human capital and ending poverty, and more of the remaining budget is spent supporting the military. As a result, the demographic transition is delayed, and population increases dramatically while prosperity grows minimally or not at all.

Comparing these scenarios and their outcomes illustrates the political challenges climate change policies face. Should we grow the economy and build the prosperity and human capital that increase our adaptive capacity? Or should we redirect some of the wealth, sacrificing some future prosperity, in order to reduce greenhouse gas emissions and slow climate change? If you have confidence in markets and human innovation to solve problems and are cautious of scientists' predictions about highly complex and uncertain systems, such as global climate, then you may prefer to grow the economy and use the increased wealth to solve climate-induced problems once they emerge. Great resources, consultants, and examples exist to assist with scenario planning and anticipating the future.[12]

Being Disruptive

The status quo might be wrong, and this might be increasingly the case as humanity advances further into the Anthropocene. Hence there might be situations where direction, alignment, and commitment need to be disrupted.

One tactic for being disruptive is to create a tension between a vision for the future and the reality of today. Use scenario planning (discussed earlier) or some other means to describe the future conditions you want to create. What would your organization or community look like in that desirable future? Compare that vision to conditions that exist today. The resulting tension could generate creative energy if it forces stakeholders to question and explain themselves. What are the assumptions and beliefs about the current and future conditions? What are stakeholder roles? What do stakeholders stand to benefit or lose? Such questioning requires self-reflection rather than repeating rote justifications from prior decisions. Self-reflection can open the opportunity for change. Moreover, the act of explaining yourself to others improves shared understanding, which can reveal or open ground where new directions can be advanced.[13]

Clearly, there are risks to being disruptive. Challenging foundational assumptions and core values makes people uncomfortable, and the challengers can be characterized as quacks and renegades to be dismissed, or threats to be managed. Most people prefer stability to change, clarity to uncertainty, and orderliness to conflict. Being disruptive requires bravery in the face of uncertainty. It means that you need the stomach to help create the space for difficult discussion and discovery to occur. Just by having that discussion you are questioning authority, increasing uncertainty, and weakening the legitimacy of things that have worked in the past. Nonetheless, the wicked challenges of the Anthropocene may demand disruptive agents, provocateurs, and opponents of the status quo.

Sharing Lessons

All aspects of adaptive leadership already reviewed in this chapter—sensemaking, learning by doing, innovating, being disruptive—require sharing lessons. The constant change and uncertainty of wicked situations produce lessons, revisions, and innovations that need to be shared if direction, alignment, and commitment are to be sustained. Stakeholders need to stay informed and on the same page, and not feel blindsided by changing roles, strategies, and expectations. Good communication plans that share lessons are an important part of leadership practices reviewed in other chapters as well, in particular collective impact (chapter 5), communities of practice (chapter 5), and partnering (chapter 6). You will see evidence of this in many of the leadership stories presented in part 3 of the book.

However, not all stakeholders need the same intensity or level of communication. The stakeholder analysis tool explained earlier in the section on sensemaking is helpful here (see Table 7.1). Stakeholders with low interest and little influence require limited attention. In contrast, actively share and shape expectations of stakeholders with much to win or lose and who can bring considerable resources to advance or stall progress. For both high-influence and high-interest stakeholders, tactics for sharing and soliciting lessons include regular intensive and expensive face-to-face meetings, teleconferences, and online platforms that maintain engagement, track progress, and store documents. For lower-influence and less-interested stakeholders, lessons can be shared through periodic press releases and social media posts.

Conclusion

How does one respond to the confounding uncertainty caused by dynamic, open systems, evolving stakeholders, and unpredictable strategies? If you become paralyzed by it and do nothing, then you continue business as usual, which is itself a decision but perhaps not a wise one. This chapter reviews strategies for dealing with this uncertainty.

Perhaps even more important than having strategies such as those reviewed in this chapter, adaptive leadership requires helping people to find the will and commitment to adapt. Dealing with failure and uncertainty requires courage and persistence. Too much change and uncertainty can be so overwhelming that people stop trying. People need to be convinced that they can make a difference. Pessimism is a self-fulfilling prophecy. We all need a sense of efficacy. Aaron Antonovsky[14] spent a lifetime studying why some people overcome adversity and uncertainty better than others. He studied people who had successfully navigated extraordinarily difficult situations, ranging from divorce and disease to the Holocaust internment. Successful people had three attributes:

(1) they made sense of and could see the challenges they faced; (2) they could assemble resources to respond; and most importantly (3) they had the will to make a difference and survive. Those without a strong sense of efficacy gave up, lost hope, and suffered or died as a result. In wicked situations, keeping hope alive, and fanning that flame in others, is an important adaptive leadership activity that anyone can practice from anywhere.

PART III

Storybook: People Practicing Wicked Leadership

CHAPTER 8

Introducing Leadership Stories

Chapters 9–15 present real-world examples of professionals and organizations applying the wicked leadership practices introduced in chapters 4–7. The purpose of this short introductory chapter is to help readers navigate those illustrations of leadership. The stories can be read independently and out of order. Table 8.1 should help you select stories to read based on the lessons you want to learn. If you want a bit more detail about each story, the table is followed by brief descriptions.

Chapter Summaries

Chapter 9. Changing Tastes: A business consultancy and nongovernmental organization (NGO) influence fickle and distracted consumers to change their diets and eat less meat. They use *identity management* techniques to persuade chefs and other foodservice professionals to use *choice editing* to alter menus and recipes in ways that reduce people's meat consumption, hence reducing the enormous environmental impacts of meat production.

Table 8.1. Navigating the Leadership Stories

Key actors	Leadership practices (chapter)	Anthropocene challenges targeted
C9: Changing Tastes: Influencing Identity and Choices for Sustainable Food		
• Foodservice businesses, professionals, and consultants • NGOs • Consumers	• Identity management (C6) • Choice-editing	• Increasing demand for food because of prosperity • Meat's environmental footprint • Circular economy
C10: Leadership Is a Key Ingredient in Water: Getting Direction, Alignment, and Commitment in India		
• NGOs • Community members • Government officials • Small businesses	• Direction (C4) • Alignment (C4) • Commitment (C4) • Train-the-trainer (C5)	• Water • Climate • Poverty
C11: Collective Impact for Climate Mitigation		
• City government • Developers • NGOs • Residents and commuters	• Collective impact (C5) • Trust (C6) • Sharing lessons (C7) • Transparency (C5) • Direction, alignment, commitment (C4)	• Climate change mitigation • Urbanization • Community energy plan
C12: Innovating Carbon Farming		
• Entrepreneurs • Farmers • NGOs • Certifiers	• Collaborative innovation (C7) • Sensemaking (C7) • Stakeholder engagement (C7)	• Climate change mitigation • Carbon capture
C13: Accounting Makes Sustainability Profitable, Possible, and Boring		
• Multinational hotel real estate investment trust • International accounting standards board	• Accountability (C5) • Transparency (C5)	• Water • Energy

Table 8.1. continued

Key actors	Leadership practices (chapter)	Anthropocene challenges targeted
	C14: Fire Learning Network	
• Federal, state, local government • NGOs • Landowners • Communities	• Community of practice and learning community (C5) • Trust (C6) • Learning (C7)	• Biodiversity • Climate
	C15: Partnering for Clean Water and Community Benefit	
• County government • Numerous businesses • NGOs	• Partnering (C6) • Accountability (C5) • Innovation (C7) • Learning (C7) • Communication (C7)	• Stormwater management • Green infrastructure • Urbanization

Chapter 10. Leadership Is a Key Ingredient in Water: An NGO helps villagers in arid and poverty-stricken regions of Rajasthan, India, create the *direction, alignment, and commitment* needed to build and restore source water management systems that dramatically improve access to water and quality of life. It uses the *train-the-trainer* strategy to amplify the impacts of limited staff.

Chapter 11. Collective Impact for Climate Mitigation: Elected city officials, city planners, real estate developers, other businesses, and local NGOs collaborate to reduce the city's greenhouse gas emissions by 75 percent. The *collective impact* strategy coordinates the actions of numerous, dispersed stakeholders and organizations with different agendas, competing and overlapping capacities, and limited tolerance for change.

Chapter 12. Innovating Carbon Farming: A group of entrepreneurs, facilitated by an NGO, engage in *collaborative innovation, sensemaking,* and *stakeholder engagement* to address one of the world's largest, but heretofore poorly managed, carbon sinks: soil. The resulting carbon farming initiative shows potential to become a major negative emissions technology and key factor in climate mitigation.

Chapter 13. Accounting Makes Sustainability Profitable, Possible, and Boring: A multinational business coordinates the actions of diverse and widely distributed stakeholders, including investors, customers, and employees located in different facilities around the world, and siloed internal divisions, such as engineering and finance. The company uses the *accountability* strategy. By reporting on implications for investment, rather than just reporting greenhouse gas emissions and water footprints, investors and other actors coordinate their actions to impact system-wide change.

Chapter 14. Fire Learning Network: A government agency is mired in inertia, skepticism, and inaction, because the paradigms of the past no longer seem to apply. In this example, the Fire Learning Network mobilizes and coordinates the actions of hundreds of actors across dozens of organizations to restore thousands of acres of habitat by managing fire differently than has been possible over the last 100 years. It uses *trust building* and *community of practice* strategies to build stakeholders' capacities to experiment, fail, and *learn by doing*.

Chapter 15. Partnering for Clean Water and Community Benefit: A county government develops a novel *partnership* with a private business that addresses floods and pollution caused when storms overwhelm its infrastructure, and provides community benefits, such as local jobs, open space, and saving tax money.

CHAPTER 9

Changing Tastes: Influencing Identity and Choices for Sustainable Food

This case study illustrates "identity management" leadership practices discussed in chapter 6, particularly triggering group membership. These leadership practices are helpful when facts alone are unpersuasive due to confirmation bias, identity protective reasoning, filter bubbles, and echo chambers. The case study also illustrates "choice editing," a strategy used to promote a circular economy by steering consumer demand to more sustainable choices. The main actors in this case are food service businesses, culinary professionals, nongovernmental organizations, and consumers. The story also illustrates a response to increased meat consumption, which presents a major challenge of the Anthropocene because of its environmental footprint.

Members of the plant-forward movement seek to produce a more sustainable food system by transforming diets and spurring innovations that create new menus, recipes, and dietary trends. Arlin Wasserman is the visionary creator and a catalyst behind the plant-forward movement, and a major actor in two organizations shaping the future of food: Changing Tastes and Menus of Change.[1]

Arlin has been working with food all his life. He grew up in a family that owned a produce company, earned graduate degrees in both natural resources and public health, held a Food and Society fellowship with the W.K. Kellogg Foundation, and was the first vice president of sustainability and corporate social responsibility at Sodexo, then the world's second largest foodservice company after McDonald's.

When Arlin worked at Sodexo, he promoted sustainable food policies and practices that were profitable for business and good for people and the planet. He coined the phrase "plant forward," which would resonate with others and galvanize action "to move meat to the edge of the plate and plants to the middle." An early effort was Sodexo's Better Tomorrow chef contest coordinated with the James Beard Foundation. The contest encouraged and rewarded chefs to create meals that "were predominantly fruits, vegetables and grains, along with modest amounts of meat, poultry and fish." The innovation and impact of Sodexo's efforts encouraged Arlin to found a consultancy, Changing Tastes, so he could advance plant-forward practices throughout the food industry.

Why plant-forward diets? Because producing meat is massively inefficient and hugely polluting. Instead of eating plants directly, we feed them to animals, wasting most of the calories as manure, heat, and greenhouse gas. A pound of grain-fed beef, for example, takes perhaps 1,800 gallons of water, half a gallon of petroleum, and almost 200 square feet of land to produce. Most of those inputs go into crops that are then fed to steers, most of which are converted to heat, belches, and manure. The cumulative impacts of eating meat cause species extinctions via habitat loss, water pollution and scarcity, and climate change. If cattle were a nation, they would be the third largest emitter of greenhouse gases, right behind the US and China.

We could consume the same calories and nutrition for a fraction of the impact by changing diets. Thus reducing meat consumption may be one of the most important and impactful strategies for sustaining development.

Efforts to advance the plant-forward diet require innovative strategies. Here we explore two pioneered by Arlin: membership identity and choice set. These strategies work because our food system is structured in such a way as to give food professionals a great deal of influence over our diets. Most of the food we eat is prepared by professionals. We eat in restaurants, order take-out, and pick up ready-to-eat food from grocery store buffets, and, when we do cook at home, we tend to use premixed packaged food rather than raw ingredients. Our food system is dominated by meals that food professionals design, mix, prepare, and serve or package. This creates enormous opportunities to influence diets because food professionals can change menus and recipes that in turn inform and change the choices consumers can and do make.

Membership Identity

Membership identity is a strategy for changing minds introduced in chapter 6. Because we humans are social creatures who want to belong to groups and be respected by others in our communities, we defend, rationalize, and become advocates for the communities we join, spreading their messages and practices. Arlin Wasserman understood that if a plant-forward community could be created within the culinary profession, its members would promote plant-forward diets and recruit others to join, thereby spreading and advancing plant-forward practices. The first key task Arlin faced was promoting membership in the plant-forward community. The second task was to empower those members to promote plant-forward diets.

He started by drawing attention to the worthwhile, socially desirable mission of promoting healthy, sustainable diets—something people would want to identify with. Getting this message to food service professionals is difficult because they are dispersed, poorly organized, and overworked. However, chefs in particular, and the food service industry generally, tend to be hyperaware of trends, popularity, rankings, and reputation. So one strategy to promote membership is to recruit charismatic and highly respected "celebrity" chefs to endorse plant-forward practices, making these practices "cool," "hip," and "in." Other chefs, restaurants, and foodies cooking at home aspire to be in the "in" group, and will do so by serving similar plant-forward entrees, recipes, and ingredients. Another membership strategy is to organize an annual gathering where members of the plant-forward community can bond, be recognized, and receive awards and recognition (one such event is organized by Menus of Change). Membership is also encouraged by promoting specific plant-forward terms that can be used with peers. Membership is signaled by using this shared jargon in menus and promotional material, and displaying logos on storefronts.

Membership is further promoted by recognizing contributions to the group. The Plant Forward Global 50 list, for example, "recognizes significant achievement in rethinking menus and traditional restaurant concepts that reflect the critical role that culinary insight and the relentless pursuit of deliciousness play in advancing health and sustainability concerns." The list recognizes professionals, restaurants, and menus elevating the role and visibility of produce, plant proteins, and other plant-based flavors. Promoting cookbooks also serves to recognize membership and reward innovation. Another way to recognize members is to organize high-profile competitions. One set of competitions organized by Menus of Change targets institutions providing dining services: hospitals, for example, compete against each other for the most sustainable, plant-forward cuisine.[2]

Promoting membership is only part of the challenge. Members also need to be empowered to promote plant-forward diets, to be advocates, to talk with customers about why a plant-forward diet is important, to explain on their menus what plant-forward goals accomplish, and to negotiate with farmers and other providers for the ingredients and supplies they purchase. In doing so, these food service professionals spread plant-forward principles. The plant-forward community provides its members with educational material, slogans, reports, and workshops that help phrase, explain, and practice plant forwardness. Perhaps the most powerful strategy among these approaches is changing the choice set.

Choice Editing

Choice editing is a strategy useful for directing consumer choices toward more sustainable options, such as will be needed to promote the circular economy discussed in chapter 3. For example, rather than try to convince fickle, distracted, disinterested retail food consumers to change what they eat, food professionals can instead change the set of choices. By editing the choice set, people act sustainably because doing so is normal, ordinary, easy, legal, and convenient. That is, people don't need to stop and think and worry about which choice is the most sustainable. They just select from a set of choices, all of which have been edited and selected by experts to be among the most sustainable possible. Menus and recipes create choice sets that determine what people eat. If the items on menus and ingredients in recipes are sustainable, then consumers of those meals will necessarily order, buy, and eat more sustainably.

The choice editors of the prepared food industry are the professionals who control menus, food merchandising, recipes, and ingredient purchasing. The following paragraphs provide some examples of things they do.

On menus, chefs can describe dishes holistically, rather than featuring the animal protein, because emphasizing meat contributes to the perception that meat is more important. Instead, descriptions on menus can make plants and meat equally enticing. Craveable and flavorful whole grains, legumes, nuts, and vegetables thus become more important components of exquisite culinary experiences. Similarly, when describing dishes, instead of using meat as a synonym for protein, chefs can instead distinguish "animal-based protein" from "plant-based protein" to help consumers understand that protein comes from multiple sources and that different sources have different impacts. Perhaps most importantly, menus can emphasize flavor rather than simply the ingredients when describing items, because research on consumer choice shows that taste trumps nearly all other attributes determining consumer choice.

Moderating portion size is another powerful choice edit because it reduces food intake as well as food waste. Advertising multiple portion sizes should be avoided, as many diners "trade up" to bigger portions, which they see as offering greater value. Menu descriptions emphasizing flavor quality over portion quantity also result in consumption of smaller portions because, as noted, taste trumps any other food attribute influencing food choice, including quantity.

Finally, retail food service professionals can encourage change throughout the supply chain. Chefs, for example, through explanations of their purchasing decisions, can advocate for and reward farmers and food producers for water-sensitive, soil-appropriate, limited-antibiotics, and other sustainable food sourcing. By ordering, requesting, and emphasizing plant-forward products specifically, and sustainably sourced food generally, food service professionals edit and shape choice sets for others up and down the supply chain, and encourage more sustainable agriculture, animal husbandry, and fisheries practices.[3]

Conclusion

Professionals who control menus, food merchandising, recipes, and ingredient purchasing, and those in the C-suite and boardroom that support or encourage them, are the choice editors of the prepared food industry. Their decisions and actions can advance sustainable food systems globally.

Food choices provide one of the most consequential leverage points for influencing sustainable development. But diet is difficult to change because food choice is grounded in cultural traditions and social values, and most importantly within the business models of the food industry that provide these prepared foods and have historically used choice set and identity management to promote meat-centric diets. The plant-forward movement uses these same strategies to recruit food professionals into the task of helping fickle, distracted, tradition-bound consumers eat sustainably, making food professionals among the most important actors in sustainable development. In Arlin Wasserman's words, "The culinary profession and the restaurant industry decide what goes on the menu and provide the choices before us. . . . Changing those choices gives consumers a safe way to try new things and decide to change their tastes, with a dash of sustainability and a smaller serving of carbon and water."

What's beyond plant-forward? Some chefs define themselves as innovators and want to be out in front of the culinary movement. They initially identified with plant-forward not just because it was good for people and the planet, but because it also was innovative. New innovations are needed because plant-forward is becoming too mainstream to satisfy the innovator's identity. Toward this end, Arlin Wasserman is using what he learned in the plant-forward movement to also promote biodiversity. He is branding the new movement as "Recovering Lost Flavors" and encouraging chefs to celebrate edible plants that have become scarce and that could be sustained as a result of market demand.

CHAPTER 10

Leadership Is a Key Ingredient in Water: Getting Direction, Alignment, and Commitment in India

This case study illustrates the most fundamental components of leadership: direction, alignment, and commitment (defined in chapter 4). It also illustrates train-the-trainer, a leadership practice that connects dispersed stakeholders (described in chapter 5). The main actors are a local nongovernmental organization (NGO) and rural villagers in Rajasthan, India. Government agency staff and businesses play minor but important roles. Finally, it illustrates responses to water scarcity, poverty, and climate change, which are major bottleneck challenges of the Anthropocene.

The Jal Bhagirathi Foundation (JBF) works in the Marwar region of the state of Rajasthan in northwestern India, one of the driest, poorest, and most densely populated places on Earth (Figure 10.1). With limited resources, JBF and its community partners generated leadership for improving water supply and sanitation projects that benefit local villages. Kanupriya Harish, the executive director, is as tireless as she is prepared. She learned about JBF in 2004 while working on her master's degree, got a job there in 2007, climbed the ranks, and became executive director in 2014. She (sort of) jokes that she always tries to be the

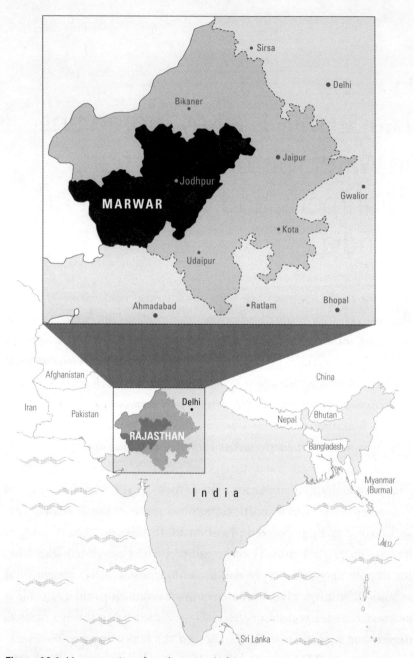

Figure 10.1. Marwar region of northwestern India.

most prepared person in the room: "What I've seen is that you lose your position because someone from below works harder and does a better job. Women have to be tougher . . . so I've prepared before I go into any meeting so I understand what I'm talking about."

Many villages in the Marwar region don't have accessible drinking water. Only a third of the villages are connected to the government's water supply, and water tables are declining several meters a year due to overextraction and climate change. Females, on average, spend 25 percent of their day fetching water for their families, which means they aren't able to attend school or engage in more economically productive activities. Already fragile rural economies and communities struggle and suffer as a result, worsening rural poverty and accelerating rural to urban migration.

As is typical of wicked challenges of the Anthropocene, solutions to this region's water challenges require collaboration among many stakeholders in different sectors. The government sector has been unable to solve this crisis by itself. Paradoxically, well-intentioned governmental efforts to improve water infrastructure and to provide relief efforts when public water systems fail have caused some villages to neglect and forget traditional water harvesting strategies, worsening the crisis in some areas. Harish explains that part of what JBF does is reimagine and apply the "dying wisdom" about water management that once sustained the region.

JBF faces the challenges common to many small NGOs: their minimal resources and staff must be amplified to have impact over a large area for a long time. Moreover, JBF must balance the need to keep its limited internal resources sharply focused on its mission while remaining flexible in how it responds to the unique social and environmental conditions of each village: a cookie cutter, one-size-fits-all approach is ineffective. JBF has been exceptionally successful, helping to create or restore over 1,500 water harvesting structures, providing almost year-long access to water for nearly 600,000 people in about 450 villages.

Water availability has increased from an annual average of four months to over ten months. The drudgery of carrying heavy loads of water on their head for long distances has been greatly reduced, empowering women to participate in other aspects of personal development and family, community, and business issues. A 140 percent reduction in the amount of income spent on purchasing water from private vendors enables families to make other investments, which has reduced poverty and increased community vitality.

Direction, Alignment, and Commitment

Direction, alignment, and commitment are the key ingredients of leadership. Good things happen when stakeholders agree on a direction or outcome they want to accomplish, align their efforts to produce that outcome, and commit to doing what's needed. As this case study illustrates, the recipe is simple in principle but difficult in practice, and when it works, the results can be life changing.

JBF has developed a process for getting small, rural, poor communities to generate direction, alignment, and commitment around water projects. The process has proven successful, replicable, scalable, and sustainable. This section explains several of JBF's tactics, first as applied to village-based projects and then as applied to JBF itself and its network of stakeholders.

Villages engage JBF by nominating themselves as being willing and ready to work on a water project. Because JBF does not have enough resources to assist every community, it employs criteria to prioritize selection, such as economic distress, ecosystem fragility, natural resources depletion, and livelihood insecurity. If a village qualifies for consideration, it is invited to form a leadership team to organize the village's effort. JBF staff coach the leadership team and mentor volunteers, but they don't plan the project. Ms. Harish explains that the village team builds leadership capacity in members and villages by requiring collaboration and coordination on "everything it takes to plan, implement, and maintain the water project."

JBF uses multiple strategies to help leadership teams achieve direction. First and foremost, it restricts the set of project choices to those related to water, rather than including a broad set of possible community development interventions, such as agriculture, entrepreneurship, education, and so on. JBF learned through trial and error that offering assistance that is too broad in scope can trigger jealousy, powerplays, and dysfunctional village dynamics, if some villagers are seen to benefit more than others (e.g., if someone's business proposal receives funding while another's does not) or if traditions are threatened (e.g., gender roles).

Mr. Prithvi Raj Singh, a founding member of JBF's board of trustees, recounts one of JBF's early efforts, in which he had supported jump-starting one woman's business. Not only did the business fail but the efforts triggered internal family dynamics and village-wide tensions about women's empowerment. The process harmed the woman's reputation, and it fueled dysfunctional factions within the community that, if anything, reduced the village's capacity to generate direction, alignment, and commitment about water—or any other topic. Learning from that and similar experiences, he adapted JBF's processes to put the onus on villagers to select and manage the project JBF invests in; that is, villagers need to produce the direction a successful project requires. JBF staff will serve only as catalysts, mentors, and resource experts; they will not make the decisions. Mr. Singh's background as a successful businessman led him to develop operating principles that still successfully guide JBF's process to promote direction, alignment, and commitment in village workgroups. Key aspects of those operating principles are illustrated throughout this case study.

Achieving direction requires a lot of work, such as deciding on the type, location, function, and timing of the water project. Achieving alignment can also prove challenging. The leadership team must recruit broad participation from the village, elect leaders, educate themselves about water traditions and technologies, decide and allocate in-kind contributions, address financial issues and establish a bank account, plan maintenance, and so on.

JBF's process also requires generating commitment from the team and the village. In early attempts, JBF fully funded the water projects but villages failed to maintain them, presumably because it was not theirs and they did not feel the responsibility of ownership. To increase a sense of ownership, commitment, and skin-in-the-game, JBF now requires communities to raise 30–50 percent of the cost of the water system. In-kind community resources can be mobilized, such as labor and materials, but significant cash contributions are expected and formalized by opening a bank account. Large contributions by a single donor are discouraged so that the community as a whole participates. Collecting and managing money also teaches financial skills, which ripple throughout the community.

Communities are further required to build and evidence commitment by forming a women's self-help group. This ensures the participation of women in project development and governance. At least 25 percent of these women must be willing to receive training from JBF so they, in turn, reach out to and organize other local women. This train-the-trainer strategy (discussed in Chapter 5) multiplies JBF's impact across the region. After a decade of doing this work, approximately 20,000 village-level volunteers have been trained, and they are now supported by approximately 100 JBF staff. JBF focuses on women's empowerment in part because it is primarily women who fetch water and thus gain the most capacity from the water project, and in part because development literature suggests that empowering women produces greater long-term benefits to the community than does empowering men.

If a village leadership team evidences direction, alignment, and commitment by achieving consensus on its plan, the proposal is submitted to a regional working group composed of JBF staff as well as representatives from neighboring villages. This group (called a block-level group, which is discussed in more detail later in the chapter), compares, evaluates, and coordinates proposals from all nearby villages. Lessons learned at the block level are shared among neighboring villages. This process further builds commitment by enhancing equity and transparency among all those engaged. If the project is approved, JBF staff work with and advise the village leadership group; but the villagers must supervise, build, and maintain the water project.

In addition to facilitating direction, alignment, and commitment within villages, JBF must, of course, facilitate direction, alignment, and commitment within its organization and across its key stakeholders. It has limited resources, and its diverse stakeholders have competing demands, so to remain effective JBF must constantly facilitate direction, alignment, and commitment. JBF operates a nested organizational structure to facilitate this outcome. At the smallest geographic level, projects are coordinated within a given village. As already described, the villages report to and are coordinated by a block-level workgroup representing the special needs and conditions of villages near one another.

Regular meetings at the block level facilitate direction, alignment, and commitment by enabling interaction between representatives from proximate villages and helping them assess the prevailing situation, voice concerns, develop strategies to counter problems, and advocate and build systems for managing and disbursing resources within the block. Direction is facilitated by getting villages on the same page with JBF goals. By sharing capacity and networking within the block level, villages are aligning their efforts and strengthening local governance. Alignment is further facilitated by getting villages and JBF to share and optimize resource allocations. Commitment is built by being transparent about decisions and sharing decision-making authority.

The block-level groups report to and are coordinated by JBF's central program management group, known as the Water Forum, which meets monthly, integrates views, and aligns efforts across the whole organization and region. Organization-wide direction is facilitated at this level because forum members are expected to contribute macrolevel expertise while remaining focused on local needs. They assist JBF in reaching outward by developing strategies and in advocating for policies with government representatives. At the next, and highest, level of JBF's nested, hierarchical organizational structure, JBF maintains an external steering group composed of experts, funders, government officials, politicians, community leaders, and representatives from other NGOs. This steering group represents the entire Marwar region and meets at least annually to review the progress made by JBF. It reviews an annual work plan that affirms JBF's direction, aligns its efforts, and builds commitment among stakeholders by providing them a platform to influence JBF's annual strategic planning.

JBF's hierarchical structure provides a network through which knowledge, influence, transparency, and vision can flow. Ms. Harish explains that "people and coordination move back and forth" between the nested levels. Many participants in the higher-level groups come from lower-level groups, so people bring forward and take back lessons, norms, vision, enthusiasm, and commitment. JBF also intentionally uses this nested structure and process to build political advocacy capacity by developing capable, empowered, conscientious citizens at local, regional, state, and national levels who can mobilize a network of actors to become a pressure group advocating for their needs.

Of course, none of this happens without great effort and organizational leadership. Visiting villages can be particularly strenuous; yet Harish mentions the joy she gets from "gallivanting" out in the field so she can learn from the villagers firsthand. She likes going alone, and often brings candies for the children as a way to share her goodwill with her partners. Conducting village visits builds the connections, trust, and open communication on which direction, alignment, and commitment depend.

Implications of Leadership

Once a community has used the direction–alignment–commitment recipe for leadership to address water, they can use it to improve sanitation, human rights, economic development, increased agricultural production, and any other outcomes they deem worthy. "Once you get the women organized around water, they tend to move on to other issues," Ms. Harish explains. An example follows.

The villagers of Potaliya depend on a rainfed pond for their livelihood and drinking water. When that pond ran dry, villagers were forced to do with less and purchase water from private vendors who delivered it in tankers at great cost, thus diverting scarce funds from more productive uses. The villagers at Potaliya approached JBF for assistance in expanding the capacity of the pond. They did so using JBF's process as described in this chapter. Of the thirty-seven-member village leadership team, thirteen were women. After successfully improving their water situation with the improved pond, the community focused its newfound leadership capacity on two other persistent problems: degraded common lands and lack of sanitation.

Village common lands are crucial to the livelihood of many who depend on livestock, but they were overrun by an invasive shrub and carved up by villagers extending their houses, fencing, and other uses into the commons. The village working group overcame local resistance and built direction, alignment, and commitment around restoring grass on common lands on which livestock could forage. Community members have subsequently benefited from the improved health of their animals, increased milk production, improved nutrition, and increased income. Furthermore, they have been able to harvest seed from some of the restored grasses and sell it to other villages. The proceeds are deposited in the new village bank account and used to address additional village needs.

The village leadership team also sought to improve sanitation. At the outset of JBF's involvement, only five households had toilets. Members of the village leadership team, with the assistance of JBF staff, organized a door-to-door survey, collecting information on sanitation practices, hygiene habits, and incidence of disease. They discussed sanitation and the need for toilets. Residents subsequently raised 50 percent of the cost for new toilets, and JBF worked with them to obtain grants to finance the remainder. Seventy-six toilets were constructed, and the village has raised its sights to seeing a toilet in every home. Aside from the positive impacts on the health of villagers, residents also express increased dignity and safety, particularly among women who now no longer need to search outdoors for private and safe places to defecate.

As this case illustrates, direction, alignment, and commitment are the key ingredients of leadership. The recipe is simple in principle but difficult in practice, and when it works, the results can be life changing.

CHAPTER 11

Collective Impact for Climate Mitigation

This case study illustrates how collective impact (introduced in chapter 5) helps coordinate the actions of widely distributed stakeholders having different agendas, competing and overlapping capacities, and limited tolerance for change. It also provides examples of accountability (chapter 5), trust (chapter 6), and continuously sharing lessons to help learn by doing (chapter 7). As any good example of leadership should, this case illustrates direction, alignment, and commitment. Elected city officials, city planners, real estate developers, other businesses, and local nongovernmental organizations (NGOs) are the key actors, collaborating to reduce their community's greenhouse gas emissions by 75 percent.

Arlington, near Washington, DC, is one of the most ethnically diverse, densely populated, and highly educated counties in the United States. It recently developed and is now implementing an award-winning Community Energy Plan that has the ambitious goal of reducing total greenhouse gas emissions by 75 percent.[1]

Rich Dooley, former weatherman and now community energy guru, was in the right place at the right time. He approached people involved to express his interest just as the planning effort started. Fortune favors the bold: a few weeks later, the initial project manager received a job offer and relocated. Rich stepped into that role, and there he remains a pivotal figure.

Rich's diverse career experiences positioned him well for coordinating the Community Energy Plan. He started as a television and radio meteorologist before shifting careers to the National Association of Home Builders, where he helped builders and developers create affordable and energy-efficient homes and sustainable communities. He also worked with the Center for Urban Policy and the Environment, where he conducted charrettes incorporating stakeholders' concerns into the decision-making process, and developed and analyzed land-use plans. Through these jobs he became knowledgeable in many fields, able to cross professional boundaries, overcome technical jargon, and find synergies where others stumbled over differences. As importantly, he is courageous enough to step outside of his professional comfort zone to engage others, take risks, and fail forward; and he is persistent enough to herd cats.

Few challenges are more daunting than climate mitigation. Meaningful impact requires connecting and coordinating countless businesses, residents, commuters, developers, building managers, energy producers, and other emitters of greenhouse gases. These stakeholders are diverse and dispersed. No one has authority over all of them. How can direction, alignment, and commitment be facilitated?

Community Energy Plans

Urban areas are the battleground where the war for mitigation will be won or lost. Urban businesses, residents, land users, and the supply chains that support them emit approximately 70 percent of all greenhouse gasses. Moreover, cities are well situated to mitigate their emissions because they have (relatively) functional governments (compared to, for example, nations), because they have wealth (they generate about 80 percent of the world's economy), and because they attract talented and motivated workers and residents. Cities, thus, have the motivation and the capacity to innovate climate solutions, and they are doing so around the world.[2] For these reasons, the US Department of Energy and other organizations support and promote community energy planning efforts. Arlington's Community Energy Plan is typical. It has six specific goals, each with specific policies, strategies, tools, and metrics:[3]

1. Increase the energy efficiency of all buildings, not just public buildings. Strategies include incentivizing developers with density bonuses for incorporating energy-efficient standards in new construction, encouraging energy reduction in existing building stock by supporting a green home program, training energy retrofit contractors, promoting energy labels on appliances, and exchanging light bulbs.

2. Promote combined-heat-and-energy systems. As much as 70 percent of energy used in electricity production can be lost as heat; if captured, it can be used to heat water and buildings. These systems also increase energy security because they still operate when regional power supplies are disrupted by events outside Arlington's borders.

3. Increase low-carbon energy options, particularly solar electric and hot water. Strategies include incentivizing developers to integrate solar into building designs and partnering with utilities to increase renewable energy powering the grid.

4. Reduce energy used in transportation. Strategies include promoting walkable, mixed-use development; mass transit; and easy access to fueling options for lower-carbon-emitting vehicles, such as electric cars.

5. Lead by example. Set and achieve targets for government facilities,

operations, and fleet vehicles that are at least as rigorous as those set for the broader community.

6. Support behavior change that reduces personal energy consumption. For example, provide residents and businesses with accessible, trusted information about energy conservation; or host green games and energy events that inspire people and organizations to acknowledge and compete to reduce energy use.

Collective Impact

Collective impact is an approach for coordinating the actions of many dispersed and diverse actors, such as what would be required to create a successful Community Energy Plan. Most successful collective impact efforts have the following five characteristics: trusted process and common agenda, shared measurement, mutually reinforcing activities, continuous communication, and backbone support. It is reassuring to note that the theory of shared leadership—direction, alignment, commitment—is clearly evidenced in these five sets of best practices. Direction is achieved by developing a shared agenda and shared measurement that clearly define objectives. Alignment is promoted through mutually reinforcing activities. Commitment is promoted by continuous communication and shared measurements that hold everyone accountable. Backbone support is probably the most overlooked component of collective impact, and hence a reason why multistakeholder efforts often fail.

The following sections illustrate these properties of collective impact using examples from Arlington's Community Energy Plan process. Rich Dooley was involved every step of the way.

A Trusted Process and a Common Agenda

Stakeholders must agree on goals they want to achieve (i.e., the direction component of direction–alignment–commitment). Frustratingly, but typical of wicked challenges such as climate mitigation, neither the problem nor the solution is known in advance of joining most collaborative efforts. Thus stakeholders must commit to collaborating before they know what, exactly, they are collaborating on (i.e., the commitment component of direction–alignment–commitment). Getting this commitment requires stakeholders to trust the process. Stakeholders need to know that their own interests will be treated fairly, that all stakeholders will be held equally accountable, and that decisions will be based on deliberation, evidence, and agreed-upon principles rather than capricious criteria or, worse, political favoritism. In chapter 6 we call this process trust, and the collective impact literature labels it a common agenda.

In the case of Arlington's Community Energy Plan, the necessary trust was facilitated by people with standing in the community who used their networks, personal relationships, and social capital to create it. We introduce these "influential champions" later in the chapter. Trust in the system was also facilitated by Rich Dooley and other staff who worked hard to maintain a transparent and responsive process.

The Energy Task Force was established to shepherd the process. Members included twenty-nine people representing a broad mix of community interests and organizations; many were CEOs of organizations, and many of the organizations were businesses. At the group's first meeting, Rich Dooley recalls introductions: "The people who are around the table hold sway in the community . . . and when they went around the table and they explained who they were, I think there was a respect around the table as to who was there, and the county meant business by assembling this group. It was an august group I would say." The only way to get such high-flying and busy people to stay engaged is to promise and maintain a trusted process.

Early discussions identified terms such as "sustainability" and "climate change" as controversial, divisive, and ambiguous. Dooley explains the reasons for concern: stories circulated about another community "that was developing an energy plan, and they got bogged down in . . . recycling water bottles or something like that. . . . It was something that was very minuscule in the big scheme of things regarding greenhouse gas emissions. But the warning was if you go down that road, you could lose the forest for the trees."

Discussion shifted to specific goals about energy security, economic competitiveness, and environmental quality. These terms generated greater and more widespread commitment, as well as more focused discussions. A strong "business case" was made during early task force meetings: businesses, residents, and the county would save money by saving energy; businesses would locate in Arlington for the competitive advantage of energy security; residents and workers would want to locate there for environmental quality; and so on.

A specific, ambitious, overarching goal emerged. In a presentation by staff and consultants very early in the process, a goal of 4.5 tons of greenhouse gas emissions per person per year was suggested as an ambitious but achievable goal. Task force members noted that Copenhagen, a world leader in climate mitigation, had a goal of 3.0 tons per person. Arlington already considered itself a leader within the US, so task force members asked staff and consultants to generate a plan and time frame for achieving a world-class goal. Dooley notes the mindset around the room at the time of the decision. "People did not achieve the status of CEO and COO and executive director by being small thinkers. These were big thinkers, these were people who would think outside the box and go for it." They were attracted to the idea of "being a shining star in the US and a beacon for others overseas." By the third month of the process, the task force agreed on 3.0 tons per person being the goal, on par with other trend-setting cities. But it took another couple years of work to agree on a plan that could achieve it.

Influential Champions

A multistakeholder effort takes time and commitment. Hence it is more likely to succeed when supported by advocates who have sufficient standing in the community to bring together key stakeholders and keep them engaged over time. The champions may be individuals, as is the case here, or respected organizations, such as universities or nonpartisan NGOs.

Rich Dooley gives kudos to elected officials serving on the County Board of Supervisors who used their networks and personal relationships to motivate key actors to participate in the planning and implementation efforts. Rich also points to real estate developers who served as critical liaisons between the planning effort, other developers, and the chamber of commerce. Rich is also quick to laud the work of the county manager, deputy, and assistant county managers who played critical roles as champions internal to Arlington's government.[4]

Mutually Reinforcing Activities

Stakeholders need clearly differentiated tasks that are coordinated to be mutually reinforcing (i.e., the alignment component of direction–alignment–commitment). They need to know what their responsibilities are, and how their individual roles contribute meaningfully to the larger outcome. Once the Energy Task Force agreed on the bold goal of 3.0 tons, it still took months of hard work to figure out how to achieve it. The business community, for example, had to agree to build energy-efficient buildings in exchange for density bonuses, and Arlington had to agree how to monitor, reward, and enforce green building standards. Similarly, civil society organizations needed to step into new roles. For example, Arlingtonians for a Clean Environment, a local NGO, agreed to take on the responsibility for managing a rebate program that incentivizes homeowners to implement residential energy efficiency improvements.

Alignment proved challenging, even within Arlington's own government operations. Arlington's administrative structure created internal silos responsible for transportation, housing, urban forestry, and environmental services. Each silo had slightly different energy-relevant operations, policy mandates, and responsibilities. At first, the Energy Task Force was ineffective at overcoming these differences. After eighteen months of work, the Energy Task Force's draft plan was rejected by Arlington's planning commission because of concerns about insufficient coordination of programs and departments internal to Arlington County's government. The task force was forced to reorganize its plan with more detailed analysis, engagement, and coordination among internal and external stakeholders, providing everyone clearer roles.

Backbone Functions

Successful multistakeholder collaborative efforts require something called a backbone to support all the other activities. These tasks are neither glamorous nor easily funded, but they are critical. They include organizing and facilitating meetings; supporting technology and communications; collecting and reporting data; writing proposals for funding; conducting research and consulting with experts; handling the myriad logistical and administrative details needed for any complicated initiative to function smoothly; and basically being responsible for facilitating direction, alignment, and commitment. Lack of a backbone infrastructure is one of the most frequent reasons why collaborative efforts fail. Some organization, or set of organizations, needed to step up to staff these critical functions. In this case, the Arlington County government committed staff and budget to the task.

Rich Dooley was one of the key vertebrae in the backbone. He organized meetings, met with stakeholders, wrote proposals, organized note taking, managed conflict, and did what needed doing to keep the process going. He is extremely attentive to the importance of an inclusive process that helps everyone to be heard and held accountable. He is also an empathic and active listener. When facilitating a group discussion or just talking one-on-one, he seamlessly paraphrases what speakers have said in attempts to make sure he and others understand. These characteristics were critical to a functioning backbone and the overall success of the collective impact process in Arlington.

Continuous Communication

Keeping everyone informed builds trust, clarifies objectives, creates motivation, and, importantly, promotes adjustments to goals and strategies as stakeholders learn from one another's successes and failures.

The task force developed a robust internal communication strategy, spearheaded by Rich Dooley, to share information, questions, and decisions. For example, questions asked by task force members and guests were meticulously recorded with attribution so that people could remember what was asked, why, and by whom. Subsequent answers or decisions related to each question were recorded and shared as a part of the public record. Dooley and other Arlington staff also worked hard to regularly meet with key stakeholders to share updates, solicit feedback, and keep everyone informed. The task force members also sought to publicize energy issues and task force efforts, holding over 100 public meetings with residents and other stakeholders. For instance, county staff, along with a bevy of volunteers, marketed and staffed a life-sized game designed to educate people of all ages and backgrounds about energy issues. And, of course, Arlington maintains a website that displayed meeting minutes and resources, and now serves as a portal for anyone interested in specifics. An implementation task force replaced the planning task force and continues to actively share information. But, as is the case with many gradually unfolding efforts, it is difficult to maintain attention, motivate, and engage stakeholders in communication efforts over the long term.

Transparent Accounting Using Shared Metrics

Measurement is where the rubber meets the road. Precise, affordable, shared metrics help collaborators get and stay aligned. Measurement with milestones defines what success and failure mean. Making these metrics transparent and accessible helps stakeholders hold one another accountable.

Arlington set a measurable overall goal of 3.0 tons of carbon dioxide equivalent per person per year by 2050. Milestones were set for 2020, 2040, and 2050 to gauge progress. Dozens of specific, measurable indicators were identified for all the subgoals that must be achieved if the larger 3.0 tons per person goal is to be realized. For example, for the strategy of increased energy efficiency in residential building stock, Arlington set milestones of reductions of 5 percent by 2020, 25 percent by 2030, 40 percent by 2040, and 55 percent by 2050 (from 2007 levels).

Despite these good intentions, Rich Dooley laments the difficulty and expense of obtaining frequent and reliable measurements. Slow progress on measurement remains a limiting factor to Arlington's implementation of its Community Energy Plan.

Secure Adequate Financial Resources

None of this would have been possible without money. Reliable funding for multiple years from at least one anchor funder is needed to support and mobilize collective impact efforts. Arlington created a reliable funding source for its energy-related initiatives using a utility tax on residential customers of electricity and natural gas. Regressivity is addressed with policies that place a greater tax on heavy users while not penalizing residents that use less than average amounts of electricity and natural gas.

The tax generates approximately $1.6 million per year. It is used to pay county staff to administer various energy programs, such as providing the critical backbone functions described earlier in the chapter, hiring outside consultants, funding energy efficiency improvements in county facilities, and supporting programs such as the Home Energy Rebates. In the years since the energy tax began, Arlington has also leveraged these funds with sources such as Energy Efficiency and Conservation Block Grant programs.

Conclusion

Connecting and coordinating the diverse and dispersed stakeholders needed to tackle wicked problems such as climate mitigation is possible with strategies such as collective impact. Success requires an inclusive, transparent, emergent, and trusted process whereby individuals and organizations understand their roles and learn by working together, including the critical but often unheralded backbone tasks.

In Arlington's Community Energy Plan, leadership by members of a county government created the conditions that collective impact requires. Critically, and encouragingly, the actions of a single individual can make a difference; in fact, without individuals practicing wicked leadership, collective impact can't happen.

CHAPTER 12

Innovating Carbon Farming

Case Overview: This case illustrates leadership practices that work in cases of confounding uncertainty where disruption is needed to reorient the status quo, reframe the situation, and bring a new order to business as usual. Specific tools include innovation, sensemaking, and stakeholder engagement (chapter 7). The main actors in this case are businesses and nongovernmental organizations (NGOs). The case also illustrates the intersection of key Anthropocene challenges: climate mitigation and agricultural productivity.

All pathways to a future that limits global warming to safe levels require removing significant amounts of carbon from the atmosphere. Soil stores about 80 percent of the world's terrestrial carbon stock, so agricultural practices that keep and increase carbon in soil are critical.

Change is difficult, however, because the agricultural system is both local and global (multiscalar), dispersed, complex, and tradition-bound. Stakeholders include farmers, food manufacturers, distributors, investors, grocers, scientists, state regulators, consumers, fertilizer and seed companies, and more. Massive uncertainty exists about how to mobilize enough stakeholders to sequester enough carbon to mitigate enough climate change. The only thing that seems certain is that the status quo must change.

Collaborative innovation offers a way forward. It is a strategy for promoting system-wide change in the face of confounding uncertainty where continuous learning, iterative testing, and refining the solutions are part of the process. This chapter describes the early stages of what might be a game changer: carbon farming. Although the innovation effort is in its early stages, it illustrates attributes of successful innovation projects: a backbone organization, a collaborative stakeholder network, bold yet specific goals, system mapping, identifying critical shifts, pivoting, and designing innovations. More details about this process and additional examples can be found at CoCreative, a consultancy with a proven process that advised on the case reported here.[1]

Collaborative Innovation

Alisa Gravitz is the CEO of Green America, a nonprofit organization that facilitates collaborations promoting socially just and environmentally sustainable societies. She is a recognized leader in solar industries, including a stint with President Carter's administration when she worked on renewable energy and energy efficiency. Alisa also has extensive experience with strategies that engage consumers, investors, and businesses in developing a more environmentally sustainable economy.

Green America's Center for Sustainability Solutions provides the administrative capacity, or "backbone," that collaborative efforts require (i.e., to organize, staff, and fund such efforts). The Center previously facilitated projects in the energy and climate, food and agriculture, financial, and labor sectors. Russ Gaskin, a principle of CoCreative and senior fellow at Green America, notes that Alisa was uniquely positioned to see the opportunity to sequester carbon through agricultural practices because of her network and her cross-sector experience with energy, climate, and agriculture.

Carbon farming will do more than mitigate climate change. Carbon farming practices improve soil health by rebuilding soil organic matter and restoring microbial diversity, which lead to increased crop productivity and restore a functional carbon cycle and topsoil creation. Healthy soils also absorb and retain more water, thus providing drought and flood resilience. In addition, healthy soils grow strong plants with deep root systems and thus reduce the need for conventional fertilizers and pesticides, helping to reduce cost to farmers as well as eliminating soil erosion and mitigating water quality problems from nutrient runoff. Thus, regenerating soil health at scale may address the problem of excess atmospheric carbon while also improving global food security, farm economics, water quality, and rural livelihoods.

Alisa's team reached out to a handful of key stakeholders to test their interest in the emerging carbon farming concept, and they found strong interest. Leveraging this early enthusiasm, Green America set out to recruit more stakeholders to participate in a *collaborative innovation network*. To communicate purpose and inspire commitment, Alisa, Russ, and colleagues drafted a clear, bold goal: "To rapidly increase the use of farming practices to sequester carbon as a major solution to the climate crisis." With this goal statement in hand, the team began interviewing stakeholders from across the agricultural value chain to identify well-connected, knowledgeable, and deeply committed stakeholders who would be inspired by the goal and willing to collaborate with others to achieve it. It is critical to recruit the right stakeholders because the innovation process requires collaborators who are representative of the larger system that the team is trying to change. Alisa explains that the "magic" of collaborative innovation happens and systemic change becomes possible with a diverse and committed group of key stakeholders.

Alisa sought network members who not only were influential in their own organizations but also had a deep personal interest in solving the bigger challenge; that is, people who could represent as well as transcend their organizations. Obviously, effective system change requires representatives from all parts of the system, including from business, NGOs, governments, academia, and community sectors. Less obviously, successful innovation efforts also need people who can simultaneously be both experts and learners. The most productive members are experts in their aspect of the system who hold a beginner's mind regarding other aspects, and are thus able to accept one another as peers who learn from and collaborate with each other. The agricultural system is so vast and complex that no one can be an expert in all aspects, so respecting and relying on others is key to success.

Good questions and careful listening are required for successful collaborative innovation. During the initial interviews, Alisa and her colleagues carefully phrased their questions to invite creativity about realistic solutions. For example, they asked, "What might it take to achieve a goal like this?" rather than, "Do you think this is possible?" The latter question asks only for evaluation, when innovation is needed. They also built engagement by asking stakeholders how their own work, priorities, and values related to the goal statement. Trust was built by active listening. From years of experience, Alisa reflects, "When you build those deep bonds of trust where people have a passion and love for the work that you're doing, as well as trust one another, it enables the network to work faster AND more deeply."

The initial interviews and assembling the network required diligence, curiosity, and time—approximately nine months. It supported a broader *sensemaking* process, discussed in chapter 7, needed to understand the system, stakeholders, strategies, and outcomes relevant to carbon farming. More specifically, Alisa and Russ had four goals:

1. Map and comprehend the larger system by identifying barriers to and opportunities for carbon farming efforts that suggest where leverage points exist.
2. Analyze stakeholders' ideas, values, interests, and assumptions regarding carbon farming, and identify those willing and able to advance this work.
3. Identify the emerging carbon farming strategies that are garnering attention and that have the potential for implementation at a scale that will reduce atmospheric carbon.
4. Outline possible and probable outcomes grounded in real human interests and constraints within the agriculture system.

Alisa and Russ assembled, through interviewing over one hundred stakeholders from across the agriculture and climate systems, a committed network of about twenty people. Alisa noted that members shared a sense of urgency about the "existential threat" of climate change and a belief that "no one can solve it alone." They also had a strong sense of urgency and commitment to "see something real happen," which facilitated collaboration, generosity, and trust, as well as real momentum.

Innovation requires goals that inspire bold thinking and specific actions. Such goals galvanize commitment, force people to think and act at scale, go beyond single solutions, and provide direction. They draw on everyone's experience, knowledge, and skills to generate energy and ownership. They should be meaningful, audacious, specific, and time-bound. Goals, like other parts of innovation, should evolve over time to continually reflect what has been learned about the situation; so it is not surprising that, early in the process, network members made a major revision to the goal statement. Initially they targeted keeping carbon below 350 ppm, but at the founder's meeting the group decided that

350 wasn't relevant to the biological realities that farmers are up against. The founders chose to go bolder, and the goal became, "To reverse the climate crisis through agricultural carbon sequestration while restoring soil health, water quality, and ecosystem biodiversity, and improving global food security, farm economics, and rural livelihoods by reducing atmospheric carbon to below 280 ppm by 2050."

The network soon made another *pivot*. Membership needed to evolve in response to changing goals and evolving understanding of the carbon–soil–agriculture system. Given the revised goal, initial members recognized that they needed to recruit additional members that could help with spreading and scaling up innovations, so they invited representatives from organizations like Cargill, General Mills, and Danone to join the network, which brought more diverse perspectives to the emerging analysis while still maintaining the powerful central goal.

The stakeholder network next turned its attention to identifying *critical shifts*, which are system changes that must happen if the goal is to be achieved. They provide focus and clarity by describing how the system needs to function in the future and what it would take to create those system functions. Critical shifts help identify specific actions that are exciting, energizing, and engaging. The network formed subteams to work on each critical shift. The subteams began designing innovations that might help create the critical shifts. The process was not linear, and there was a lot of pivoting. Alisa and Russ facilitated brainstorming and ideation using "old-fashioned as well as some new-fangled" techniques, such as brainstorming-in-a-box, intuition pumps, impact-feasibility maps, and other methods, to generate the most powerful and promising set of ideas. Subteams built their top ideas into concrete "initiative concepts" that would lead to specific outcomes associated with the critical shift. The teams then quickly prototyped, tested, and then redesigned these concepts. Redesigns were initially based on feedback from the rest of the network, and then from stakeholders outside but impacted by the redesign and thus key to making the critical shift occur. Six initiatives emerged, each with its own subteam committed to making it happen.

1. Midwest Grains—Shift five million additional acres of corn/soy cropland to rotational small grains and cover crops for building soil health; develop new markets for small grains; rapidly replicate in other regions.

2. Drawdown Dairy—Revise dairy production to reduce methane emissions and increase carbon sequestration by shifting feed and forage, adopting advanced soil health practices, and making changes in herd and crop genetics.

3. Soil Superheroes—Build a platform and movement to reach twenty to forty million people with the inspirational story of how soil health is the solution right beneath our feet that can reverse the climate crisis and improve global food security, water quality, human health, and economics for rural communities. Spotlight the farmers, scientists, companies, and others leading this movement.

4. Mighty Microbes—Introduce large-scale conventional growers to the benefits of soil health through no-risk trials. Demonstrate improved value creation and return on investment from the use of management systems that regenerate healthy biodiverse soil microbial communities that boost crop productivity by providing nutrients naturally and reducing the need for chemical inputs, providing an important on-ramp to rapid scaling of carbon farming.

5. Rewarding Farmers—Develop financial rewards for farmers sequestering carbon and financing for their transition to new practices.

6. Soil Carbon Standard—Develop and promote a standard for measuring carbon sequestration and evaluating soil health so that everyone in the supply chain is using the same language and measures. The standard can also be used to reward farmers for their success and to incentivize investments in carbon farming strategies.

Next we describe two of these initiatives in more detail: Soil Carbon Standard and Soil Superheroes.

Work on the Soil Carbon Standard illustrates the importance of being flexible and willing to pivot as new information becomes available. At the beginning of the innovation exercise, most network members did not want to develop a new carbon accounting system because they believed too many already existed, and new standards and certifications would be redundant and ineffective. However, Alisa and Russ were able to facilitate discussion around what was *needed*, rather than what was *not wanted*. What was needed was the ability to assure people across the value chain that carbon was actually being sequestered, so that farmers could be incentivized and rewarded. The Soil Carbon Standard group prototyped a possible accounting system. Once the rest of the network agreed that the standard was strategically important, the initiative team raised funding and engaged NSF International, an organization that develops and monitors standards, to lead the technical development of what is now known as the Soil Carbon Index, which is currently being piloted.

At the time of this writing, the Soil Carbon Index is being tested in the supply chains of network members, including leading brands, NGOs, and investors who are keen to give it a try and help refine it so it will work for their needs. The subteam is recruiting additional farms for the 2020 growing season, hiring dedicated staff, and launching a significant fundraising effort to support rolling out the initiative. The subteam also holds regular group calls to share updates, and it schedules in-person workshops to bring members together for learning, connecting, and shaping the actions that they will advance together. These meetings bring experts and practitioners together to discuss topics ranging from financial and policy aspects of carbon farming to lessons from key innovators in other industries who have designed rapidly scalable training and technical programs.

The Soil Superhero initiative group provides another example of an initiative to produce a critical shift that builds a movement supporting regenerative agriculture. The first part of the larger social media campaign promotes the stories of farmers applying carbon farming practices. The stories are designed to build consumer demand that will push corporations to invest in shifting their purchasing to farms using regenerative forms of production. In addition to posting profiles on websites, network members agreed to a collective social media campaign targeting deep into their value chain and consumer pool. One current proposal is to motivate consumer action to encourage state-level policy makers to enact and fund healthy soils and carbon farming policies.

Fifth-generation farmer Rick Clark from Williamsport, Indiana, is an example of a Soil Superhero.[2] In his story he talks about "stacking" multiple carbon farming practices on many of his 7,000 acres, including "no till" planting that can seed a farm without turning the soil or exposing stored carbon to oxidation, planting diverse cover crops that build nutrients in the soil, and allowing livestock to graze and fertilize the fields. Clark plants something he calls "gunslinger" in the fall, before the next spring's planting of corn and soy. It includes five cover crops that each perform a necessary function for soil health: Haywire forage oats build biomass to protect the soil; sorghum Sudan grass promotes the growth of beneficial mycorrhizal fungi; tillage radish helps break up compacted soil; and Austrian winter peas and balansa clover add nitrogen, an essential nutrient. Then, in the spring, Clark plants corn and soybeans directly into the cover crops, a practice he calls "farming green."

"We will not plant our corn or soybean crops unless it is into green growing cover crops," he says. Clark defines soil health simply as "decreasing inputs and increasing yield." His practices not only increase soil carbon but also help to reduce weeds and insects, reducing the need for chemical pesticides and saving Clark as much as $600,000 a year on inputs.

Conclusion

This chapter provided a glimpse into an ongoing and perhaps game-changing innovation of climate mitigation: sequestering carbon in soil though agriculture. Carbon farming, to be successful at scale, requires multiple simultaneous interventions in different parts of the agricultural system. This requires coordination of countless diverse and distributed actors; not just farmers, but also investors, distributors, certifiers, regulators, and consumers. To accomplish this system change, the collaborative innovation network assembled by Alisa is in it for the long term: "We're working together to advance initiatives that will help deliver on the important key shifts needed to move the system toward a future where we have achieved our big goal."

Although unfinished, these efforts to promote carbon farming illustrate attributes of successful collaborative innovation efforts. The carbon farming network has adopted bold goals: reducing atmospheric carbon to below 280 ppm by 2050 while promoting farming communities. They have built a network of people who are knowledgeable and influential in their organizations, who are willing and able to think beyond their organizational perspective, and who trust each other enough to collaborate deeply. They have facilitated sensemaking to create a shared understanding of the whole system. They have identified critical shifts that can cause system-wide change. They have learned and pivoted to adjust to new information and other forces acting on the system. They are supported by a backbone organization that facilitates long-term relationships with a transparent process. In summary, they have led from where they are without authority to generate direction, alignment, and commitment among stakeholders by connecting, collaborating, and adapting.

System-wide change becomes possible when the right stakeholders are assembled and are engaged in a collaborative process for innovation with good facilitators like Alisa and Russ.

CHAPTER 13

Accounting Makes Sustainability Profitable, Possible, and Boring

This case study illustrates accountability, a leadership strategy introduced in chapter 5, that coordinates actions of people who might not meet nor know they are connected. Key actors are a multinational business, a non-profit organization, investors, accountants, customers, and employees located in different facilities around the world. The story also illustrates efforts to reduce greenhouse gas emissions and water footprints.

Make sustainability "boring." That's what we need to do, according to Brian Macnamara, senior vice president and controller at Host Hotels & Resorts. Brian has over twenty-eight years of experience in accounting, finance, and real estate. It's a tongue-in-cheek plug for his profession, accounting, which he thinks many people assume is boring. But if accountants can measure sustainability, then people can be accountable for managing it, and the world becomes more sustainable.

Host Hotels & Resorts is the world's largest real estate investment trust and one of the largest owners of luxury and upper-upscale hotels. As part of its commitment to quality, Host has embraced sustainability as a core aspect of its business and is regularly recognized as a leader in sustainability.[1] To further their initiatives and influence others, Host began working with the Sustainable Accounting Standards Board (SASB) in 2017.

Michael Bloomberg, the founder of Bloomberg LP and former mayor of New York City, apparently agrees with Brian. He supports SASB, a nonprofit founded in 2011 to facilitate communication between companies and investors. Bloomberg explains his support on SASB's website: measuring sustainable impacts "will bring significant financial benefits to investors and help strengthen the overall economy." Investors and other market actors need to assess sustainability-related risks and opportunities, and SASB "is trying to fill the need of giving comparable information on sustainability issues." It is not enough just to report water use or carbon emissions; investors and managers need to see how these measures are material to investment decisions and how companies are managing these challenges.

The goal of SASB is to have companies use common metrics in their annual Form 10-K reporting to the US Securities and Exchange Commission (SEC). Form 10-K reporting differentiates SASB from other green accounting practices because it is publicly available, informs investment decisions, and carries legal liability. Thousands of lawyers, finance professionals, and government regulators (Brian calls them the Enforcers) audit and, if necessary, litigate, forcing companies to report accurate information relevant to investment decisions. While this extra scrutiny would seem to discourage sustainability reporting, it does the exact opposite because the reports guide investment decisions (i.e., companies are making green decisions because it adds to the bottom line). Brian explains: "Companies and their investors now look at sustainability measures as a positive rather than a burden."

Brian explains Host's motivations: "We wanted to brag about all the smart sustainability money being spent on infrastructure at our hotels and prove that it was making a difference to the bottom line. We invest to make money for our shareholders, so we wanted to demonstrate the return on our sustainability investments. Investments such as LED lights, water-saving fixtures, solar panels, co-generation plants, gray-water recycling, etc., all contribute to annual savings." Brian also notes that "in the hospitality business, it is also what our guests expect." Host also wanted to be out in front, helping design the metrics so the reports actually produce sustainability impacts, like energy and water savings, and are supportable and defensible for a public company. Because SASB sustainability metrics are not required by the SEC, not every company reports them. However, reporting may become more common as SASB works with the Financial Accounting Standards Board and the SEC to drive standardized, reliable, and auditable metrics for all industries.

Host is already transparent about many sustainability impacts. It publicly reports on common sustainability metrics, such as the Carbon Disclosure Project and the Global Reporting Initiative, but it believes SASB's indicators have greater "materiality" to investment outcomes. Brian explains: "Host's environmental engineers may be delighted with building retrofits that reduce long-term energy and water use and lower long-term operating costs. However, year-over-year savings may be relatively small, so every project must meet a return on investment threshold as well as create sustainable benefits."

Over the last four years, Host's efforts to reduce energy and water usage have resulted in an average of $7 million annually of permanent cost reductions. However, those year-over-year changes may be immaterial to a property's value. For example, if the building is sold several years after a retrofit, energy and water savings may not translate into a meaningful return on investment for Host. Even more importantly, Host needs comparable measures that help prioritize sustainability-related risks or opportunities, which might not be water or energy savings but rather the height above sea level of a resort's infrastructure or the availability of water in a drought-prone location. Investors want information that is material to company performance and return on investment, not just information about energy use and water footprints. Seen in this light, sustainability investment decisions are more about ensuring future returns through thoughtful design and management. Thus Host's innovations in SASB accounting and 10-K reporting not only have the potential to substantively change business practices promoting sustainability but also ensure the long-term viability of the company.

"How we did this is much more difficult than why," Brian recalls. "Whatever we report must first meet our own internal high standards in addition to external auditing standards and avoidance of legal liability issues." Brian explains that "the single most challenging issue to reporting is defining what constitutes sustainable investing." For example, Host hired third parties to verify utility usage, and then adjusted the results for differences in heating and cooling days and changes in utility rates, because they wanted to assure an apples-to-apples comparison consistent with other financial performance metrics. Brian poses a few hypothetical questions to help explain the accounting challenge: "Which of the following is a sustainable investment: painting a roof white, installing energy-efficient cooling towers, or covering a roof in Hawaii with solar panels? Arguably the answer is yes to all three, but what if we needed to paint the roof, or replace the cooling units, or the local government required us to source power sustainably? Is it still sustainable investing or just required maintenance, and does how we define it matter to investors?" SASB reporting helps define sustainable investing and align the goals of investors with specific sustainability practices and outcomes that are material, measurable, and comparable.

Getting direction and alignment around this effort required the commitment of Host's C-suite. Ultimately, they led the charge. There was plenty of reason for caution, Brian recalls, especially from colleagues who asked, "Why report something we're not legally required to report when investors may not consider it worthwhile?" Generating the needed commitment meant developing and reaching agreement on the appropriate disclosures to minimize liability while emphasizing the economic benefit and proving to external auditors that the data were accurate. The use of scientific methods and the engagement of third parties to audit the data helped, but, ultimately, the personal commitment of many people within and outside Host was required. Host's reputation as a savvy investor in lodging real estate has been carefully cultivated. It works closely with and relies on the managers of its properties, like Marriott and Hyatt, to drive sustainable results. Host's reputation as a sustainability leader has been increasingly noted in its press releases, board presentations, and other outlets, so Host wanted to ensure that reputation and to protect against the liability of being targeted as misleading or greenwashing. SASB reporting supported all of these goals and outcomes.

SASB reporting efforts have already paid off. The company recently issued the first green bond in the lodging industry, raising $650 million of capital from investors. SASB reporting and innovations are noted in Host's annual reports and presented to their trade group, the National Association of Real Estate Investment Trusts. Other companies now use features of Host's 10-K reporting in their own 10-K reporting. "Plagiarism is the highest form of flattery in the boring world of accounting," Brian smiles. One unexpected benefit is that SASB accounting provided the common language that helped Host's internal departments, siloed by their own metrics and cultures, communicate, evaluate proposals, and coordinate action. SASB reporting broke down some of the silo barriers, got people talking, and created cross-department synergies that led to common goals to improve sustainability, management efficiency, and return on investment.

Brian offers a final plug for his professional identity as an accountant: "The public shouldn't have to guess what investments are sustainable or how they impact the bottom line. Running a company sustainably isn't just about doing the right thing, it's doing the smart thing. We need to support organizations like the SASB that establish and require rules to allow comparability between companies. We need to apply those rules consistently in documents that carry risk, such as the 10-K, and then let investors evaluate if the investments are material and add value to the company. Basic accounting. Boring. But I believe boring will be what drives long-term success in sustainability."

Conclusion

Solving wicked challenges of the Anthropocene requires coordinating the actions of geographically and temporally dispersed actors, some of whom will never meet nor know they are connected, such as Host's investors and facility managers. Accountability offers a strategy. Non-profits like SASB help implement it. Once you know what to look for, you'll see accountability strategies everywhere, including consumer-facing labels on products that tout sustainability, certification systems, commodity roundtables, and public reports of deforestation and pollution. In this case study, we examined how accountability is used to influence business-to-business and business-to-investor relationships. The theory is intuitive: measuring and reporting impacts make people and organizations more accountable for their actions. But as with other leadership practices that are simple in principle, they are difficult in practice and require innovation, hard work, and perhaps some risk of being boring.

CHAPTER 14

Fire Learning Network

The Fire Learning Network mobilizes and coordinates thousands of actors across hundreds of organizations to reduce fire risks, and to restore thousands of acres of habitat that are increasingly impacted by climate change and other Anthropocene challenges. It illustrates multiple leadership strategies, including community of practice (introduced in chapter 5), single- and double-loop learning (introduced in chapter 7), and trust building (introduced in chapter 6). The main actors are government agency personnel from local, state, and national levels who were mired in inertia, skepticism, and inaction; and The Nature Conservancy, an international nongovernmental organization (NGO), that organized a learning network to facilitate direction, alignment, and commitment to action.

Fire is a charismatic example of a wicked Anthropocene challenge. It destroys suburbs, burns forests, releases carbon dioxide, and renews ecologies. It also adapts to changing human land development patterns and ignores political, disciplinary, and professional boundaries.

Until recently, wildland fire management in the United States has been stuck in a "rigidity trap," perpetuating programs and responses that worked in the past.[1] For much of the twentieth century, natural resource professionals sought to control and extinguish all fire because doing so was thought to increase predictability and productivity of forest, livestock grazing, water supplies, and other resources, which in turn would promote economic development, which in turn would promote public health, prosperity, and democracy. But the programs and practices that sought to control fire ended up creating conditions for catastrophic and unanticipated fires that severely damaged property, forests, human health, and economies. A century of fire suppression changed species composition, tree density, and fuel levels to the point that fires could no longer be controlled. Wildfires began burning longer, hotter, and farther, disrupting the economy and governance, and costing billions of dollars. A new approach was needed.[2]

The US Fire Learning Network (FLN) helped generate the direction, alignment, and commitment needed to overcome inertia and restore fire to many landscapes. It coordinated discussions and actions of fire professionals from 650 different organizations by creating a network for fire professionals to interact. It helped them collaborate to restore fire as an accepted socioecological process to hundreds of thousands of acres.

Like many leadership strategies, the FLN is simple in principle but nuanced in practice. This chapter uses examples from the FLN to illustrate a few specific leadership practices that make the network so successful: community of practice, learning, and trust. Other leadership practices contributed to its success and accomplishments, but these three are among the most important and relative to wicked leadership.

Community of Practice on Steroids

A learning network is structured like a community of practice, a leadership strategy reviewed in chapter 5 that promotes learning by practitioners, from practitioners, about their practices, so that they can become more effective and influential. The FLN has all the attributes of a successful community of practice. It is participatory, accessible, relevant, funded, and staffed. It also goes beyond typical communities of practice and provides coaching, mentoring, face-to-face meetings, and, importantly, expectations to develop collaborative projects. Details of these attributes are described as follows:

Participatory—Participants voluntarily join and commit time (they may receive some financial support for travel to meetings). Participants set the geographic boundaries that define their region, define the issues needing attention, and identify the topics/focus of occasional face-to-face meetings.

Accessible—Participants ask questions of the network using multiple entry points: listserv, phone list, face-to-face meetings, and by directing inquiries to moderators who are tasked to find and share the requested information.

Relevant—FLN's currency is relevant information that helps people do their jobs and hence promotes career success. It focuses on collecting and sharing information about fire relevant to the local and regional landscapes where professionals work.

Funded and staffed—Coordination, moderation, and vision are all required to provide timely information, promote quality control, and hold participants accountable for participation in collaborative efforts. The US Forest Service provided the initial seed money to fund and staff the FLN, and other agencies and organizations subsequently contributed to operational expenses, but The Nature Conservancy provides the initiative, staffing, and know-how that make learning networks succeed.

Coaching and mentoring—Professionals learn from others who have been through similar situations. The FLN pairs experienced fire professionals with novices to mentor them through a process for planning, burning, and monitoring.

The FLN is a nested and hierarchical network (Figure 14.1). A landscape unit is the lowest level of the hierarchy. It is composed of people who work in a geographically defined area and thus share similar ecological and cultural challenges and properties, such as past fire history, invasion by nonnative species, agricultural crops and practices, and political jurisdictions. The bulk of the work and most of the learning occur at this smallest unit of the FLN. Participants collaborate virtually but also meet several times a year to develop their own plans for burning, get feedback on those plans, interact with experts they respect, share ideas and resources, and socialize and get to know one another as individuals rather than just as representatives of their organization. Still, fire is a large-scale socioecological force, so the landscape networks cover vast areas (the median size is over 400,000 acres) and include multiple ownerships—public and private.

Regions form the next level of FLN's hierarchy and are composed of proximate landscapes. There are eleven regions across the US. Since landscapes within a region share similar characteristics and challenges, moderators of a regional network focus activities on sharing and comparing plans and lessons from across the region. They also help find and share experts, mentors, and other resources most relevant within that region.

The third level of the hierarchy is the nation. The national staff provide general vision and funding, and they gather and share lessons relevant across regions and to all network participants. The result of this coordinated, moderated, hierarchical network is a powerful learning tool that also promotes direction, alignment, and commitment to managing and restoring fire.

Learning

As the name implies, the Fire Learning Network (FLN) facilitates learning. By design, it provides a vehicle for sharing tacit, experiential knowledge

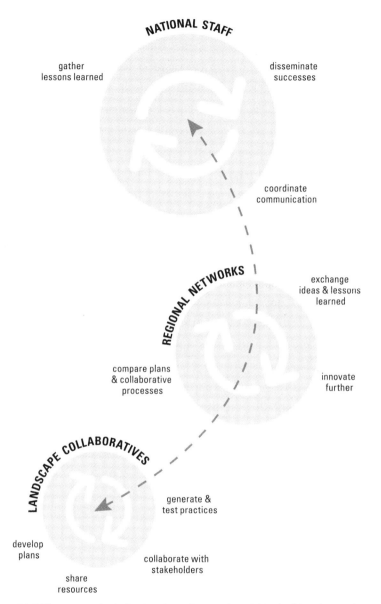

NATIONAL STAFF

gather
lessons learned

disseminate
successes

coordinate
communication

REGIONAL NETWORKS

exchange
ideas & lessons
learned

compare plans
& collaborative
processes

innovate
further

LANDSCAPE COLLABORATIVES

generate &
test practices

develop
plans

collaborate with
stakeholders

share
resources

Figure 14.1. Three nested, reinforcing tiers of network activities build and spread capacity to promote biodiversity and change institutional norms. (Adapted from "Fire Learning Network Field Guide," The Nature Conservancy, 2012, http://www.conservation gateway.org/documents/fln_fieldguide_vmarch2012_rev29apr12_web.pdf.)

not easily captured in academic books, courses, and studies. Here we focus on single-loop and double-loop learning introduced in chapter 7.

You are likely familiar with single-loop learning that follows the intuitive plan–do–check–fix procedure introduced in chapter 7. FLN landscape-level groups facilitate this type of learning. FLN participants are expected to assess what worked and what failed from each fire they manage. Lessons are then shared throughout the network, either as reports, advice, or field trips to the sites. During landscape-level meetings among peers, network participants share stories about techniques they applied, point out problems with particular approaches that arise under specific ecological or social conditions, and suggest alternative techniques based on their field experience. They also share lessons for overcoming organizational and social barriers, such as obstructionist bosses and foot-dragging communities.

Single-loop learning helps improve answers to tactical questions, such as how and where to burn. Double-loop learning improves our questions and focuses more on strategy. It is a bit less intuitive, but perhaps more powerful and important because a poor answer to a good question can be more helpful than a good answer to a poor question.

FLN facilitates double-loop learning by creating a safe space for participants to question the status quo: people share and unpack assumptions about the role and frequency of fire, why to introduce it, and the paradigmatic differences between introducing fire and preventing it. By facilitating better questions, the network builds capacity in individuals and has likely contributed to a larger paradigmatic change in land management agencies.

Trust

Part of FLN's success results from nurturing the trust that helps people collaborate, share, and change. Recall from chapter 6 that trust has three attributes that can be managed: rational, affinity, and process.

Rational trust is promoted by perceptions of competence and past performance. It is rational to trust individuals who competently and consistently deliver on their promises. FLN members prove both their competence and their commitment by answering questions that other members submit to the network. Also, network members are assigned coaches with deep expertise and experience. These highly competent professionals commit considerable time to mentoring and thereby build rational trust throughout the network. Trust is further enhanced because participants within a landscape-level network are required to review one another's project work in a timely manner, thus delivering on promises to offer constructive feedback. In addition, the network serves as a trusted source of state-of-the-art science and practice because that information is vetted by moderators before being posted and shared.

Affinity trust is based on feelings of social connectedness, positive shared experiences, and shared identities. Members of FLN occasionally meet face-to-face, and these meetings always include time for social interaction, both formally during field trips and informally through sharing meals and drinks, allowing participants to get to know one another as people, not just as professionals representing different organizations. Group identity is enhanced by naming the group (i.e., the Great Plains FLN or the California Klamath-Siskiyou FLN), distributing hats, shirts, and other swag with FLN logos, and rewarding commitment to the network with funded trips to regional and national meetings. Further, participants are given opportunities to share their own, specific "war stories" about fire, and thus personalize their experience with feelings as well as their own expertise.

System/process trust requires that the process by which decisions are made and membership is granted be deemed fair, transparent, and consistent. FLN's facilitators create clear ground rules requiring best practices of active listening, respecting others, and meeting management.

These facilitators set transparent expectations for performance, and they hold members accountable. Moreover, each landscape-level network has considerable member-driven control over its work, ensuring that facilitators, employers, and sponsors can't steer the group, thereby empowering collective ownership, creativity, and self-direction.

Conclusion

Managing fire requires collaborative, connective, adaptive leadership. Fire literally and figuratively crosses contentious political, organizational, and professional boundaries. Fire managers must continually adapt, learn, and respond to the unique and dynamic characteristics of each landscape and region. They must collaborate to address policy and regulatory barriers. They must share resources and expertise. And they must commit to the shared goal and broader cause of restorative fire. The FLN enables all of this, in part, by applying leadership practices such as community of practice, single- and double-loop learning, and trust.

CHAPTER 15

Partnering for Clean Water and Community Benefit

This case study illustrates best practices for forming and maintaining partnerships.[1] As described in chapter 6, formal partnerships help organizations coordinate the resources needed to address large-scale Anthropocene challenges and opportunities. Some of the best practices for partnership illustrated here appear as leadership practices elsewhere in the book: accountability and continuous communication (in chapter 5), and learning by doing, innovation, and sharing lessons (in chapter 7). The main actors in this story are a county government, for-profit businesses, and churches. The story also illustrates strategies for green infrastructure, specifically source- and stormwater management.

Roads, roofs, lawns, and other (nearly) impervious surfaces make rain a problem. They prevent groundwater recharge, cause floods, and carry pollution that creates dead zones. Heavy rains can overwhelm concrete storm drains, wastewater treatment plants, and other gray infrastructure engineered to manage stormwater. Green infrastructure can be part of the solution. It uses bioswales, retention ponds, tree canopies, and countless other designed natural features to hold and filter rain where it falls rather than letting it rush off to cause problems. There is a catch: bidding, designing, building, and maintaining infrastructure—green or gray—are difficult and expensive tasks that can overwhelm any organization, even a government.

Prince George's County (PGC), Maryland, had a goal of installing approximately 15,000 acres of green infrastructure to meet Chesapeake Bay clean water targets. But the cost and time needed to do it in-house exceeded budgets and deadlines. So PGC partnered with a private company, Corvias Solutions, using an innovative model known as a Community-Based Public–Private Partnership designed to help communities expedite the delivery of needed infrastructure plus additional community, economic, and environmental benefits that otherwise would not be affordable. The resulting partnership, known as the Clean Water Partnership, is the first public–private partnership of its kind or scale.[2]

This case study illustrates the nuances of successful partnerships by introducing readers to this innovative approach to managing stormwater.

Partnering

Partnering is a formal type of collaboration, useful when organizations collaborate so closely that their reputations become interdependent. It is hard work (ask anyone in a relationship). If you can solve a problem yourself, just do it. Partner only when it is worth the effort, as is likely when attempting to tackle large-scale challenges, such as water, climate, urbanization, or countless other pressing challenges of the Anthropocene. This partnering story illustrates several best practices introduced in chapter 6.

Innovation

Partnerships often require and produce innovative thinking, which clearly happened in this case. The traditional approach to siting, design-ing, constructing, inspecting, and maintaining stormwater infrastruc-ture is based on the design–bid–build–bid–operate model of project delivery. This segmented approach limits the capacity of government agencies to build and maintain stormwater infrastructure efficiently and quickly, in part because the costs associated with each phase get inflated when contractors offer low bids to obtain contracts, but then use change orders due to unknown/unforeseen site conflicts, design errors, and var-ious other problems. Because design, construction, and maintenance are not integrated, designers may make suggestions that make construction more expensive and maintenance difficult. Likewise, costs cut during construction may make operations more expensive.

The innovation in this case was to combine the siting, design, permit-ting, construction, maintenance, and financing. This more-integrated approach minimizes the need and cost of change orders. It incentivizes designers and contractors at each phase, such as siting and construction, and reduces costs that occur later in time, like operations, hence reducing overall cost rather than just the cost of construction. The Clean Water Partnership also innovated financial tools to speed project implemen-tation and billing, provide access to private capital, and better manage risks. It also helped local small businesses acquire necessary skills to com-pete for the work and removed bureaucratic barriers to their participa-tion, such as high levels of legal paperwork and long delays in payment.

Governance and Accountability

Partnerships need good governance structures that minimize misunder-standings. Accountability, the leadership practice discussed in chapter 5, forces partners to construct and use mutually agreed-upon metrics to evaluate outcomes, report those evaluations, accept responsibility for actions producing those outcomes, and be responsive to sanctions from partners for those actions. Making those reports visible to all partners encourages them to be accurate, timely, accessible, and trusted.

Before the Clean Water Partnership was formed, the county issued a "request for qualifications," seeking a company that could make a long-term commitment, promote the county's goals, and deliver and manage stormwater infrastructure. Corvias Solutions was selected as having these qualifications. The county and Corvias then worked for eighteen months to spell out the partnership's governance in a master program agreement that details deliverables and expectations for the first three years and a master maintenance agreement that details deliverables and expectations for the next 30 years. These governance agreements describe Corvias's compensation structure, which is performance based, with a base fee for the successful implementation of all projects and an incentive fee for meeting all socioeconomic goals. Corvias receives payment only if completed projects produce the specified outcomes.

Performance is evaluated against milestones, such as generation and delivery of functioning retrofitted acres, adherence to the scheduled construction timeline and budget, and achievement of socioeconomic goals. Socioeconomic goals include 30 percent of the labor being locally sourced, and over 40 percent of the businesses being local, small, and owned by veterans, minorities, persons with disabilities, or women. Accountability and trust are enhanced by an independent, third-party "completion certifier" who assesses and reports on key outcomes. Further, the county maintains a public-facing dashboard available on its website that documents key outcomes.

Fill Key Roles

Different roles become critical at different stages of partnering, including champions, brokers, managers, and external advocates.

Champions use their personal and professional reputations to promote the partnership's credibility and profile during its early stages, giving potential partners confidence that investments of time and reputation will be worthwhile. PGC had several internal champions, including the economic development officer, chief financial officer, and county executive. One key champion was Mr. Coffman, deputy director for the Department of the Environment. He advocated for a new way of designing and constructing green infrastructure that drove down costs; increased the pace of project implementation; and integrated design, construction, and maintenance efforts. Another key champion, Mr. Adam Ortiz, director of the county's Department of Environment, also advocated for the project within the county government and with resident organizations because he felt the benefits of a novel partnership outweighed the risks of deviating from business as usual: "We determined that it is riskier to continue doing things the same way . . . versus trying something different."

Brokers act on behalf of the partners to construct the partnership's foundations by creating a compelling vision, clear expectations, and transparent accounting, as well as making sure the necessary, mundane, practical, day-to-day activities are carried out. A broker often works at one of the partnering organizations. Greg Cannito, managing director with Corvias Solutions, performed this function. He kept parties engaged and on track during the negotiations that produced the overarching program and maintenance agreements.

Managers provide a steady, reliable presence to manage partnership projects and communications. Managers assimilate, winnow, record, and distribute information critical to keeping partners informed, engaged, and trusting the partnership. They identify and select projects in a manner consistent with the public interest, manage contractors, ensure best practices, and ensure inspection and maintenance programs. Once the partnership was brokered, Greg Cannito stayed on with Corvias to work alongside PGC staff to manage the partnership.

External advocates provide legitimacy, expertise, and perhaps funding needed to maintain partner engagement during the initial, tenuous stages. External advocates also provide a political counterbalance to external critiques of the partnership. The Clean Water Partnership had many advocates. For example, Ms. Dominique Lueckenhoff, the acting director of the Water Protection Division of EPA Region 3, advocated the community-based partnership model, organized conferences on the topic, and helped PGC engage the necessary experts. Also, the county is fortunate to have located within its boundaries a nationally recognized nongovernmental organization promoting green infrastructure and related technologies: Low Impact Development Center. Its principal and founder, Neil Weinstein, served as an external advocate, providing a respected professional voice. Once the project began, religious institutions in the county also became important advocates and created a critical mass of early projects that demonstrated viability and credibility. As noted later in the chapter, local religious organizations also became important external advocates at the critical early stages of the project.

Respect and Utilize Partners' Differences and Strengths

Partners, especially coming from different sectors (i.e., business, government, and civil society), may struggle to understand one another's priorities, resources, procedures, strengths, and risks. A business partner, for example, has skills for managing supply chains and labor, while a government partner has the power to convene and tax. Partners from different sectors also worry about different risks to reputation, autonomy, and resources.

PGC, as a government agency, brought regulatory authority and funding. It implemented a stormwater fee and bond program to generate funding. It also used its power of convening to bring stakeholders to the table. In addition, PGC focused attention on jobs, economic development, environmental quality, and other community-oriented benefits over and above mere compliance with stormwater regulations. However, by contracting with a private business to plan and organize its green infrastructure efforts, the county risked negative public perceptions that they were abdicating control over public goods and misusing public treasure.

Corvias brought traditional business strengths of project management, technical skills, and established supply chains. Corvias had public–private partnership experience and a reputation, built in California managing military housing. It earned a reputation of being able to fix problems faster than the military paperwork was able to identify and report the problems. While much of the engineering for stormwater infrastructure is similar around the country, local conditions present unique design–build–operation challenges. Therefore, Corvias contracted with local businesses to leverage local knowledge and networks to the advantage of the Clean Water Partnership.

Establish Shared Goals and Mutual Benefit

Clear, trusted, robust discussion is needed to share, understand, and shape the partnership's goals. To be sustainable, the partnership must provide specific benefits to each partner.

County officials needed to meet the regulatory requirements imposed on the county by the state, and to show that they did so at a cost and quality better than traditional procurement would allow, and at an acceptable risk. The Clean Water Partnership met these goals. It produced significant short-term savings, including quicker issuing and better enforcement of permits and more efficient administration of billing and finance. The county also benefited by transferring risk and expense of long-term operations to Corvias, who assumed responsibility for long-term maintenance. Additionally, the Clean Water Partnership made PGC a trendsetter among local jurisdictions, boosting its reputation. The partnership also contracted with local, small businesses that were owned by minorities, veterans, persons with disabilities, and women, as well as implemented a mentor–protégé program for the local workforce. Moreover, a cluster of local companies is emerging that can service surrounding counties by implementing green infrastructure.

Corvias was motivated by the promise of steady funding that mitigates risks from variabilities in political elections and business cycles. They also sought to build a reputation for using infrastructure projects to provide community benefits, a market niche they see expanding nationally.

Churches and other religious institutions have a powerful political voice in the county. They were concerned about the county's stormwater programs because they had substantial impervious surfaces (parking lots and roofs) and were being charged a stormwater fee. Corvias reached out to them early, installing green infrastructure projects on their properties that reduced their stormwater fees and provided amenity and educational benefits for their members. These organizations then became early backers that gave the county some political cover to stand up and demonstrate the Clean Water Partnership.

Learning Culture with Continuous Communication

Successful, enduring partnerships learn from their successes and mistakes; that is, they learn by doing. Many activities of any partnership are novel and outside the scope of an organization (that is why the partnership was formed) and thus can be viewed as an opportunity for learning that enhances partners' knowledge, skills, practice, and reputation. True collaboration transforms partners by helping each partner grow.

The Clean Water Partnership succeeded, in part, because both the county and Corvias embraced a culture of learning and adapting. The clear milestones and regular reporting created opportunities for the county and Corvias to evaluate progress, adjust practices, and refine expectations. County administrators remained flexible and open to adjustments. Corvias knew they had a lot to learn. They had experience managing complex community partnerships managing infrastructure, but not green infrastructure, and not in PGC. They needed to learn quickly, not just the green infrastructure technologies appropriate for PGC but also the marketing and sales approaches appropriate for PGC landowners. So they hired local contractors and local experts in green infrastructure, and they adopted and rewarded an internal culture and decision-making process that explicitly recognized the need to learn and adapt quickly.

Conclusion

Partnerships are difficult and risky, but increasingly they are required to tackle wicked challenges of the Anthropocene that exceed the capacity of any single organization to solve. The Clean Water Partnership illustrates how, properly designed and carefully executed, a partnership benefits all parties and provides a better outcome, at less cost, in less time. Importantly, this case illustrates that public–private partnerships can recognize, produce, and monitor community benefits. In addition to installing functioning green infrastructure in less time and at lower cost, the ongoing partnership is producing local jobs, building local business capacity, and improving citizen engagement.

CHAPTER 16

Conclusion

The challenges of the Anthropocene are wicked, exceeding the wisdom, vision, and authority of individual people and organizations. Whole systems must change, which requires mobilizing many diverse and loosely connected stakeholders while trying to navigate great uncertainty and dynamism. Changing these systems requires connecting across scales, collaborating across differences, and adapting to uncertainties—the wicked leadership practices described and illustrated in this book.

Practicing wicked leadership can be challenging if you are a technically trained professional or scientific expert. In wicked situations, your credibility and efficacy will depend less on the depth of your technical expertise and more on the leadership skills that allow you to put your expertise, and the expertise of others, into action. You must influence and collaborate with stakeholders using different agendas, standards, and approaches.

The Anthropocene creates another dilemma for professionals and experts, who tend to be risk averse and rely on the tools and skills they've been trained and certified to use. These conservative tendencies produce the outcome captured by the adage: if your only tool is a hammer, everything looks like a nail. This conservatism presents a dilemma because the challenges of the Anthropocene can't be solved using only our current tools and thinking. Individual expertise, which focuses vertically within silos (or ruts), must be merged with leadership skills that work horizontally across sectors and professions. Problem solvers must shift from a technical mindset that seeks certainty to a collaborative mindset that respects diversity of perspective. Rather than seek control, experts must see interactions and interdependencies. Rather than strive for solutions that prevent failure, they must adopt strategies to learn from muddling through, repeated trial and error, and rapid piloting and pivoting. Rather than avoiding system interventions for fear of unintended consequences, they must recognize that not acting is in itself an act that carries the same responsibility as acting.

The time for impact and relevance is now. Wicked leadership skills and practices can help you impact system-wide change. Hopefully, you are willing to tackle the Anthropocene's wicked challenges (the book is written to you). If so, your inner voice is likely raising yet another dilemma. While being flattered by the suggestion that you can change the world, you recognize that you're already struggling to keep up with your own responsibilities, and it seems unfair to saddle you with the additional burden of leadership. Nonetheless, the burden rests on you. Accept it. Indeed embrace it. Many can do a little, some can do a lot, and together we can sustain development.

An Invitation

The book's first section provided a roadmap, charting some of the biggest challenges and opportunities of the Anthropocene and how they will shape the careers of sustainability professionals. How will you position yourself to have impact and relevance?

The book's second section described leadership tools and strategies that work on wicked challenges of the Anthropocene. Will you try a few and lead from where you are? Will you work to generate direction, alignment, and commitment to help stakeholders connect, collaborate, and adapt?

The book's third section shares stories of people, not too different from yourself, who made a difference by applying leadership practices described in this book. What will be your story?

Humanity stands on the cusp of great challenge and great opportunity. We have the tools to respond. Our future looks bright, but only if more of us help. Will you?

Notes

Chapter 1: Introduction

1. Hans Rosling, *Factfulness* (New York: Flatiron Books, 2019).

Chapter 2: Challenges of the Anthropocene

1. Jeremy Davies, *The Birth of the Anthropocene* (Oakland: University of California Press, 2016); Will Steffen et al., "The Anthropocene: Conceptual and Historical Perspectives," *Philosophical Transactions of the Royal Society of London A: Mathematical, Physical and Engineering Sciences* 369, no. 1938 (2011): 842–867, https://doi.org/10.1098/rsta.2010.0327.

2. Anthony J. McMichael, "Insights from Past Millennia into Climatic Impacts on Human Health and Survival," *Proceedings of the National Academy of Sciences* 109, no. 13 (2012): 4730–4737, https://doi.org/10.1073/pnas.1120177109; William James Burroughs, *Climate Change in Prehistory: The End of the Reign of Chaos* (Cambridge, UK: Cambridge University Press, 2005).

3. Other versions of this optimistic, glass-half-full vision include Hans Rosling, *Factfulness: Ten Reasons We're Wrong about the World—and Why Things Are Better Than You Think* (New York: Flatiron Books, 2018); S. Pinker, *Enlightenment Now: The Case for Reason, Science, Humanism, and Progress* (New York: Penguin, Random House, 2018); Eric W. Sanderson, Joseph Walston, and John G. Robinson, "From Bottleneck

to Breakthrough: Urbanization and the Future of Biodiversity Conserva-tion," *BioScience* 68, no. 6 (June 2018): 412–426, https://doi.org/10 .1093/biosci/biy039.

4. Darrell Bricker and John Ibbitson. *Empty Planet: The Shock of Global Population Decline* (New York: Crown, 2019); M. Roser, "When Will the World Reach 'Peak Child?'" Our World in Data, February 8, 2018, https://ourworldindata.org/peak-child; K. Riahi et al. "The Shared Socio-economic Pathways and Their Energy, Land Use, and Greenhouse Gas Emissions Implications: An Overview," *Global Environmental Change* 42 (2017): 153–168, https://doi.org/10.1016/j.gloenvcha.2016.05.009. For a less rosy scenario, see Patrick Gerland et al., "World Population Stabi-lization Unlikely This Century," *Science* 346, no. 6206 (2014): 234–237, doi: 10.1126/science.1257469.

5. Edan Prabhu, "How Will We Cope When There Are Too Few Young Peo-ple in the World?" Brookings, October 10, 2017, https://www.brookings .edu/blog/future-development/2017/10/10/how-will-we-cope-when -there-are-too-few-young-people-in-the-world/.

6. Homi Kharas and Kristofer Hamel, "A Global Tipping Point: Half the World Is Now Middle Class or Wealthier," Brookings, September 27, 2018, https://www.brookings.edu/blog/future-development/2018/09/27 /a-global-tipping-point-half-the-world-is-now-middle-class-or-wealthier/; Michael Spence, *The Next Convergence: The Future of Economic Growth in a Multispeed World* (New York: Picador, 2011).

7. Kishore Mahbubani, *The Great Convergence: Asia, the West, and the Logic of One World* (New York: PublicAffairs, 2013).

8. Rob Dellink, Jean Chateau, Elisa Lanzi, and Bertrand Magné, "Long-Term Economic Growth Projections in the Shared Socioeconomic Path-ways," *Global Environmental Change* 42 (2017): 200–214, https://doi .org/10.1016/j.gloenvcha.2015.06.004.

9. Jeffrey D. Sachs, *The Age of Sustainable Development* (New York: Colum-bia University Press, 2015).

10. The century-old relationship between prosperity and urbanization may be breaking. Urbanist Richard Florida summarizes the challenge in *The New Urban Crisis: How Our Cities Are Increasing Inequality, Deepening Segregation, and Failing the Middle Class—and What We Can Do About It* (New York: Basic Books, 2017). "The nub of the global urban crisis is this," Florida writes, "in the midst of the greatest urban migration in

human history, urbanization has ceased to be a reliable engine of progress." Globalization has disrupted the connection between cities and their surroundings. No longer do adjacent rural areas benefit by providing resources and labor to their cities. Instead, resources and talent come from around the globe. Florida's concerns have merit, and warrant attention to how well all urban citizens can take advantage of the wealth and prosperity that cities generate and concentrate. For example, skyrocketing real estate prices make urban areas less accessible to people without means, diminishing access to opportunity and increasing inequality.

11. Tim Searchinger, Richard Waite, Craig Hanson, and Janet Ranganathan, "Creating a Sustainable Food Future: A Menu of Solutions to Feed Nearly 10 Billion People by 2050," World Resources Institute, 2018.

12. UN Sustainable Development Goal 6.

13. Arjen Y. Hoekstra and Pham Q. Hung, "Globalisation of Water Resources: International Virtual Water Flows in Relation to Crop Trade," *Global environmental change* 15, no. 1 (2005): 45–56.

14. Peter Schulte, Stuart Orr, and Jason Morrison, "Shared Risks and Interests," in *The World's Water*, ed. Peter Gleick (Washington, DC: Island Press, 2014), 19–33.

15. CDP Global Water Report 2017, https://www.cdp.net/en/research /global-reports/global-water-report-2017.

16. Alex Epstein. *The Moral Case for Fossil Fuels* (New York: Penguin, 2014).

17. "World Energy Outlook 2018," International Energy Agency, https:// www.iea.org/reports/world-energy-outlook-2018.

18. "WEO 2015 Special Report: Energy and Climate Change," International Energy Agency, https://webstore.iea.org/weo-2015-special-report-energy -and-climate-change.

19. "Emissions Gap Report 2019," UN Environment Programme, https:// www.unenvironment.org/resources/emissions-gap-report-2019.

20. Vaclav Smil, *Making the Modern World: Materials and Dematerialization* (West Sussex, UK: John Wiley & Sons, 2014); Peter Lacy and Jakob Rutqvist, *Waste to Wealth* (London: Palgrave Macmillan, 2015); Anke Schaffartzik et al., "The Global Metabolic Transition: Regional Patterns and Trends of Global Material Flows, 1950–2010," *Global Environmental Change* 26 (May 2014): 87–97, https://dx.doi.org/10.1016%2Fj.gloen vcha.2014.03.013.

21. Richard Dobbs, James Manyika, and Jonathan Woetzel. *No Ordinary Disruption: The Four Global Forces Breaking All the Trends* (New York: PublicAffairs, 2015).

22. Kishore Mahbubani, *The Great Convergence: Asia, the West, and the Logic of One World* (New York: PublicAffairs, 2013).

23. OECD, *In It Together: Why Less Inequality Benefits All* (Paris: OECD Publishing, 2015), http://www.oecd.org/social/in-it-together-why-less -inequality-benefits-all-9789264235120-en.htm; Jesse Bricker, Alice Henriques, Jacob Krimmel, and John Sabelhaus, "Measuring Income and Wealth at the Top Using Administrative and Survey Data," *Brookings Papers on Economic Activity* 2016, no. 1 (Spring 2016): 261–331; United Nations, "Leaving No One Behind: The Imperative of Inclusive Development. Report on the World Social Situation 2016," 2016, https://www .un.org/development/desa/dspd/world-social-report/rwss2016.html.

24. Anne Case and Angus Deaton. *Deaths of Despair and the Future of Capitalism*. (Princeton, NJ: Princeton University Press, 2020); Benjamin M. Friedman, *The Moral Consequences of Economic Growth* (New York: Random House, 2005); OECD. *In It Together*; Grigoli, Francesco. "A New Twist in the Link between Inequality and Economic Development," International Monetary Fund, 2017, https://www.imf.org/external/pubs /ft/sdn/2011/sdn1108.pdf.

Chapter 3: Opportunities of the Anthropocene

1. According to the 2019 EHS&S Salary Survey (https://www.naem.org /what-we-offer/research/reports/read/2019-ehs-sustainability-salary -report), the average annual salary of employees in this field is approximately $100,000 (EHS&S stands for Environmental, Health, Safety, and Sustainability). And, salaries have increased in recent years. The Green-Biz State of the Profession Report finds that, on the high end, directors and vice presidents in corporate sustainability have gained increased pay, status, and influence.

2. Richard Dobbs, James Manyika, and Jonathan Woetzel, *No Ordinary Disruption: The Four Global Forces Breaking All the Trends* (New York: PublicAffairs, 2015); Business & Sustainable Development Commission, *Better Business, Better World*, 2017, http://report.businesscommission .org/uploads/BetterBiz-BetterWorld_170215_012417.pdf; "The Transformation of Growth: How Sustainable Capitalism Can Drive a New Economic Order," Generation Foundation, 2017, https://www.genfound

.org/media/1436/pdf-genfoundwp2017-final.pdf; Peter Lacy and Jakob Rutqvist, *Waste to Wealth: The Circular Economy Advantage* (London: Palgrave Macmillan, 2015).

3. UNEP, "Fostering and Communicating Sustainable Lifestyles: Principles and Emerging Practices," 2016, http://wedocs.unep.org/handle/20.500 .11822/17016; Andrew J. Hoffman, "The Next Phase of Business Sustainability," Stanford Social Innovation Review, 2018, https://ssir.org /articles/entry/the_next_phase_of_business_sustainability.

4. Steering Committee of the State-of-Knowledge Assessment of Standards and Certification, *Toward Sustainability: The Roles and Limitations of Certification* (Washington, DC: RESOLVE, Inc., 2012); Sarah Iweala et al., "Buy Good, Feel Good? The Influence of the Warm Glow of Giving on the Evaluation of Food Items with Ethical Claims in the U.K. and Germany," *Journal of Cleaner Production* 215 (2019): 315–328.

5. Amy Brown, "Sustainable Investing At All-Time High, Says Morgan Stanley," TriplePundit, published September 17, 2019, https://www.triple pundit.com/story/2019/sustainable-investing-all-time-high-says-morgan -stanley/84916; Larry Fink, "A Fundamental Reshaping of Finance," BlackRock, 2020, https://www.blackrock.com/corporate/investor -relations/larry-fink-ceo-letter.

6. Bruce Kahn and Marc Fox. "Linking Climate Engagement to Financial Performance: An Investors Perspective," Sustainable Insight Capital Management and CDP, 2013, https://www.sicm.com/docs/CDP_SICM _VF_page.pdf; Jody Grewal, Clarissa Hauptmann, and George Serafeim, "Stock Price Synchronicity and Material Sustainability Information," Harvard Business School Working Paper, 17-098, May 2017.

7. S. K. Yazinski, "Strategies for Retaining Employees and Minimizing Turnover," HR.BLR.com. 2009, https://hr.blr.com/whitepapers/Staffing -Training/Employee-Turnover/Strategies-for-Retaining-Employees-and -Minimizing-.

8. "Millennials at Work: Reshaping the Workplace," PWC, 2011, https:// www.pwc.de/de/prozessoptimierung/assets/millennials-at-work-2011 .pdf; Deloitte, Global Millennial Survey, 2020, https://www2.deloitte .com/global/en/pages/about-deloitte/articles/millennialsurvey.html; David Lubin and Daniel Esty, "The Sustainablity Imperative," *Harvard Business Review*, May 2010.

9. Business & Sustainable Development Commission, *Better Business, Better*

World"; Connie A. Van der Byl and Natalie Slawinski, "Embracing Tensions in Corporate Sustainability: A Review of Research from Win-Wins and Trade-Offs to Paradoxes and Beyond," *Organization & Environment* 28, no. 1 (March 1, 2015): 54–79.

10. Andrew McAfee, *More from Less* (London: Simon & Schuster, 2019); Andrew Winston, *The Big Pivot: Radically Practical Strategies for a Hotter, Scarcer, and More Open World* (Brighton: Harvard Business Review Press, 2014).

11. Michael Bloomberg and Carl Pope, *Climate of Hope: How Cities, Businesses, and Citizens Can Save the Planet* (New York: St. Martin's Press, 2017); Allie Goldstein, Will R. Turner, Jillian Gladstone, and David G. Hole, "The Private Sector's Climate Change Risk and Adaptation Blind Spots," *Nature Climate Change* 9 (2018): 18–25.

12. Denise Gül Holzendorff, "Living on the Coke Side of Thirst: The Coca-Cola Company and Responsibility for Water Shortage in India," *Journal of European Management & Public Affairs Studies* 1, no. 1 (2013): 33–36.

13. Paul Ekins and Nick Hughes, *Resource Efficiency: Potential and Economic Implications*, UNEP, 2017, https://www.resourcepanel.org/sites/default/files/documents/document/media/resource_efficiency_report_march_2017_web_res.pdf; Peter Lacy and Jakob Rutqvist, *Waste to Wealth: The Circular Economy Advantage* (London: Palgrave Macmillan, 2015); Richard Dobbs, James Manyika, and Jonathan Woetzel, *No Ordinary Disruption: The Four Global Forces Breaking All the Trends* (New York: PublicAffairs, 2015).

14. WEF & PACE, "New Circular Vision for Electronics: Time for a Global Reboot," World Economic Forum, 2019, https://www.weforum.org/reports/a-new-circular-vision-for-electronics-time-for-a-global-reboot.

15. Terry Yosie, "The Circular Economy at the Inflection Point," GreenBiz, 2017, https://www.greenbiz.com/article/circular-economy-inflection-point.

16. "What Is a Circular Economy?" Ellen Macarthur Foundation, 2017, https://www.ellenmacarthurfoundation.org/circular-economy/concept.

17. Oran R. Young, *On Environmental Governance: Sustainability, Efficiency, and Equity* (Boulder: Paradigm Publishers, 2013).

18. Saskia Sassen, *Territory, Authority, Rights: From Medieval to Global Assemblages* (Princeton, NJ: Princeton University Press, 2006).

19. W. D. Eggers and P. Macmillan, *The Solution Revolution: How Business, Government, and Social Enterprises Are Teaming Up to Solve Society's Toughest Problems* (Cambridge, MA: Harvard Business Review Press, 2013).

20. Mariëtte van Huijstee and Pieter Glasbergen, "NGOs Moving Business: An Analysis of Contrasting Strategies," *Business & Society* 49 (2010): 591–618; Tim Forsyth, "Panacea or Paradox? Cross-Sector Partnerships, Climate Change, and Development," *Climate Change* 1, no. 5 (September/October 2010): 683–696.

21. Steering Committee of the State-of-Knowledge Assessment of Standards and Certification, *Toward Sustainability: The Roles and Limitations of Certification*, RESOLVE, Inc., Washington, DC, 2012, https://www.resolve.ngo/docs/report-only.pdf.

22. Magali A. Delmas and Oran R. Young, eds. *Governance for the Environment: New Perspectives* (Cambridge, UK: Cambridge University Press, 2009); Anand Giridharadas, *Winners Take All: The Elite Charade of Changing the World* (New York: Alfred A. Knopf, 2018).

23. Bloomberg and Pope, *Climate of Hope*; Bruce Katz and Jeremy Nowak, *The New Localism: How Cities Can Thrive in the Age of Populism* (Washington, DC: Brookings Institution Press, 2018).

24. Benjamin R. Barber, *Cool Cities: Urban Sovereignty and the Fix for Global Warming* (New Haven: Yale University Press, 2017); "A Pathway to Sustainable American Cities: A Guide to Implementing the SDGs," UN Sustainable Development Network, 2019, http://unsdsn.org/resources/publications/a-pathway-to-sustainable-american-cities/.

25. William B. Meyer, *The Environmental Advantages of Cities: Countering Commonsense Antiurbanism* (Cambridge, MA: MIT Press, 2013).

26. Eric W. Sanderson, Joseph Walston, and John G. Robinson, "From Bottleneck to Breakthrough: Urbanization and the Future of Biodiversity Conservation," *BioScience* 68, no. 6 (2018): 412–426.

27. "The Smart and Sustainable City," Government of Dubai, accessed June 27, 2020, https://u.ae/en/about-the-uae/digital-uae/smart-sustainable-cities.

Chapter 4: Leadership Basics

1. Many leadership theories and practices exist. A respected overview can be found in Peter Northouse, *Leadership: Theory and Practice*, now in its eighth edition. The specific theory, language, and logic of wicked

leadership used here borrow heavily from work by Drath and colleagues; Wilfred H. Drath et al., "Direction, Alignment, Commitment: Toward a More Integrative Ontology of Leadership," *Leadership Quarterly* 19, no. 6 (2008): 635–653.

2. For an overview of the traditional leader–follower theory of leadership see W. Bennis, "The Challenges of Leadership in the Modern World: Introduction to the Special Issue," *American Psychologist* 62, no. 1 (2007): 2–5; M. Shriberg, "Sustainability Leadership as 21st-Century Leadership," in *Environmental Leadership: A Reference Handbook*, ed. D. R. Gallagher (Los Angeles: Sage, 2012), 469–480; Peter G. Northouse, *Leadership: Theory and Practice*, 7th ed. (Los Angeles: Sage, 2015).

3. Horst W. J. Rittel and Melvin M. Webber, "Dilemmas in a General Theory of Planning," *Policy Sciences* 4, no. 2 (1973): 155–169; Bryan G. Norton, *Sustainable Values, Sustainable Change: A Guide to Environmental Decision Making* (Chicago: University of Chicago Press, 2015); Ronald A. Heifetz, *Leadership without Easy Answers* (Cambridge, MA: Harvard University Press, 1994); Keith Grint, "Problems, Problems, Problems: The Social Construction of 'Leadership,'" *Human Relations* 58, no. 11 (2005): 1467–1494.

4. Kelly Levin, Benjamin Cashore, Steven Bernstein, and Graeme Auld, "Overcoming the Tragedy of Super Wicked Problems: Constraining Our Future Selves to Ameliorate Global Climate Change," *Policy Sciences* 45, no. 2 (2012): 123–152.

Chapter 5: Connecting across Space and Time

1. Aarti Gupta, "Transparency under Scrutiny: Information Disclosure in Global Environmental Governance," *Global Environmental Politics* 8, no. 2 (2008): 1–7; Rüdiger Hahn and Michael Kühnen, "Determinants of Sustainability Reporting: A Review of Results, Trends, Theory, and Opportunities in an Expanding Field of Research," *Journal of Cleaner Production* 59 (2013): 5–21.

2. Andrew Spicer and David Graham Hyatt, "Walmart Tried to Make Sustainability Affordable. Here's What Happened," *The Conversation*, August 13, 2018, https://theconversation.com/walmart-tried-to-make-sustainability-affordable-heres-what-happened-76771.

3. Arthur P. J. Mol, "The Future of Transparency: Power, Pitfalls and Promises," *Global Environmental Politics* 10, no. 3 (2010): 132–143.

4. Jerome Bruner, "The Narrative Construction of Reality," *Critical Inquiry* 18, no. 1 (1991): 1–21; Jerome Bruner, *Making Stories: Law, Literature, Life* (Cambridge, MA: Harvard University Press, 2002); Chip Heath and Dan Heath, *Made to Stick: Why Some Ideas Survive and Others Die* (New York: Random House, 2007); Stephen Denning, *Squirrel Inc.: A Fable of Leadership through Storytelling* (San Francisco: John Wiley & Sons, 2004); Michael F. Dahlstrom, "Using Narratives and Storytelling to Communicate Science with Nonexpert Audiences," *Proceedings of the National Academy of Sciences* 111, Supplement 4 (2014): 13614–13620, https://www.pnas.org/content/pnas/111/Supplement_4/13614.full.pdf.

5. D. Taylor, *The Healing Power of Stories: Creating Yourself through the Stories of Your Life* (New York: Doubleday, 1996).

6. Five classic references address why and how to construct powerful stories: Bill Birchard, "Once Upon a Time," Strategy+Business, April 10, 2002, https://www.strategy-business.com/article/18637?gko=4b582; Stephen Denning, *The Leader's Guide to Storytelling: Mastering the Art and Discipline of Business Narrative* (San Francisco: John Wiley & Sons, 2005); Heath and Heath, *Made to Stick*; Randy Olson, *Don't Be Such a Scientist* (Washington, DC: Island Press, 2009), 1226, 1228; Terry Pearce, *Leading Out Loud: A Guide for Engaging Others in Creating the Future* (San Francisco: John Wiley & Sons, 2013).

7. This story is adapted from A. Simmons, *The Story Factor: Secrets of Influence from the Art of Storytelling* (Cambridge, MA: Perseus, 2001).

8. Etienne C. Wenger and William M. Snyder, "Community of Practice: The Organizational Frontier," *Harvard Business Review*, January–February 2000, 139–145.

9. June Holley, *Network Weavers Handbook* (Athens, OH: Network Weaving Publishing, 2012); Peter Plastrik, *Connecting to Change the World* (Washington, DC: Island Press, 2016).

10. IUCN, "Join the Rights-Based Approach to Conservation Portal," August 5, 2010, https://www.iucn.org/content/join-rights-based -approach-conservation-portal.

11. The World Bank Group, "Communities of Practice Questions and Answers," www.worldbank.org/archive/website01006/WEB/IMAGES /COP_QA.DOC.

12. John Seely Brown and Paul Duguid, "Balancing Act: How to Capture

Knowledge without Killing It," *Harvard Business Review*, May–June 2000.

13. Bruce Goldstein, *Transformative Learning Networks: Guidelines and Insights for Netweavers*, Network of Stem Education Centers, accessed June 27, 2020, https://www.aplu.org/projects-and-initiatives/stem -education/stem-education-centers-network/Goldstein_paper.pdf.

14. At least four types of scaling exist. "Quantitative scaling" or "scaling out" is expanding, customizing, and sustaining successful programs to reach a greater number of people in different places and over time. "Functional scaling" broadens and extends the functions of a project to include more impacts, such as adding nutrition to a literacy campaign. "Political scaling" refers to expansion through influence of the political process. And "organizational scaling" refers to expansion of the organization implementing the innovation. Often these four dimensions are interrelated and interdependent. We focus here on quantitative scaling—distributing innovations and solutions so they reach more people in more places.

15. Larry Cooley and Richard Kohl, "Scaling Up—from Vision to Large-Scale Change: A Management Framework for Practitioners," Management Systems International, 2006, http://www.msiworldwide.com /approach/tools/scaling-up-framework-toolkit/; A. Hartmann and J. F. Linn, "Scaling Up: A Framework and Lessons for Development Effectiveness from Literature and Practice," Brookings Global Economy and Development. Washington, DC: Brookings Institution Wolfensohn Center for Development, 2008; WHO, "Beginning with the End in Mind: Planning Pilot Projects and Other Programmatic Research for Successful Scaling Up," Geneva, Switzerland: World Health Organization, 2008, Expandnet.net; Susan H. Evans and Peter Clarke, "Disseminating Orphan Innovations," *Stanford Social Innovation Review* 9, no. 1 (2011): 42–47.

16. Everett M. Rogers, *Diffusion of Innovations*, 3rd ed. (New York: The Free Press, 2010).

17. FSG, for example, is a mission-driven consulting firm for leaders in search of large-scale, lasting social change: http://www.fsg.org/ideas-in-action /collective-impact; John Kania and Mark Kramer, "Collective Impact," *Stanford Social Innovation Review* 74 (2011); Community Tool Box, "Collective Impact," University of Kansas, https://ctb.ku.edu/en/table -of-contents/overview/models-for-community-health-and-development /collective-impact/main.

18. There are four excellent summaries of information campaigns that affect behavior change: Doug McKenzie-Mohr, "Promoting Sustainable Behavior: An Introduction to Community-Based Social Marketing," *Journal of Social Issues* 56, no. 3 (2000): 543–554; Anja Kollmuss and Julian Agyeman, "Mind the Gap: Why Do People Act Environmentally and What Are the Barriers to Pro-environmental Behavior?" *Environmental Education Research* 8, no. 3 (2002): 239–260; T. Compton, *Common Cause: A Case for Working with Cultural Values*, WWF-UK's Strategies for Change Project, September 2010, https://assets.wwf.org.uk/downloads/common_cause_report.pdf; Community Toolbox, "Social Marketing," University of Kansas, https://ctb.ku.edu/en/sustain/social-marketing/overview/main.

Chapter 6: Collaborating across Differences

1. See also Nobel Laureate Sen, who critiques the logic of economic theory that assumes a rational, economic man, concluding that "the purely economic man is indeed close to being a social moron" (336) in Amartya K. Sen, "Rational Fools: A Critique of the Behavioral Foundations of Economic Theory," *Philosophy & Public Affairs* 6, no. 4 (1977): 317–344. Other ways to explain the two distinct types of cognitive processing include system 1 and system 2 or central and peripheral processing. See Richard E. Petty and John T. Cacioppo, "The Elaboration Likelihood Model of Persuasion," in *Communication and Persuasion*, ed. Richard E. Petty and John T. Cacioppo (New York: Springer, 1986), 1–24.

2. Yochai Benkler, Robert Faris, and Hal Roberts, *Network Propaganda: Manipulation, Disinformation, and Radicalization in American Politics* (Oxford: Oxford University Press, 2018).

3. Dan M. Kahan, Ellen Peters, Erica Cantrell Dawson, and Paul Slovic, "Motivated Numeracy and Enlightened Self-Government," *Behavioural Public Policy* 1, no. 1 (2017): 54–86; A. Tuschman, *Our Political Nature: The Evolutionary Origins of What Divides Us* (Amherst: Prometheus Books, 2013); Lilliana Mason, *Uncivil Agreement: How Politics Became Our Identity* (Chicago: University of Chicago Press, 2018).

4. The most adamant climate deniers, for example, tend to be highly educated. Within their echo chambers, these people are pressured and rewarded to be thought leaders. P. J. Henry and Jaime L. Napier, "Education Is Related to Greater Ideological Prejudice," *Public Opinion Quarterly* 81, no. 4 (12 December 2017): 930–942, https://doi.org/10.1093/poq

/nfx038. An interview with Taylor can be found at Reckonings, http://
www.reckonings.show/episodes/category/climate-change.

5. K. H. Jamieson and J. N. Cappella, *Echo Chamber: Rush Limbaugh and
the Conservative Media Establishment* (Oxford: Oxford University Press,
2008); Lilliana Mason, "Ideologues without Issues: The Polarizing Consequences of Ideological Identities," *Public Opinion Quarterly* 82, no. S1
(11 April 2018): 280–301, https://doi.org/10.1093/poq/nfy005.

6. Masahiro Matsuura and Todd Schenk, eds., *Joint Fact-Finding in Urban
Planning and Environmental Disputes* (New York: Routledge, 2017).

7. Craig E. Runde and Tim A. Flanagan, *Becoming a Conflict Competent
Leader: How You and Your Organization Can Manage Conflict Effectively*,
2nd ed. (San Francisco: John Wiley & Sons, 2012).

8. George Lakoff, "Why It Matters How We Frame the Environment,"
Environmental Communication 4, no. 1 (2010): 70–81.

9. Brendan Nyhan and Jason Reifler, "The Roles of Information Deficits
and Identity Threat in the Prevalence of Misperceptions," *Journal of Elections, Public Opinion and Parties* 29, no. 2 (2019): 222–244.

10. Chris Ernst and Donna Chrobot-Mason, *Boundary Spanning Leadership:
Six Practices for Solving Problems, Driving Innovation, and Transforming
Organizations* (New York: McGraw Hill Professional, 2010).

11. Kristin Hurst, Marc J. Stern, R. Bruce Hull, and Danny Axiom, "Address-
ing Identity-Related Barriers to Collaboration for Conservation through
Self-Affirmation Theory and Moral Foundations Theory," *Conservation
Biology* (October 29, 2019), https://doi.org/10.1111/cobi.13428.

12. Craig E. Runde and Tim A. Flanagan, *Developing Your Conflict Competence: A Hands-on Guide for Leaders, Managers, Facilitators, and Teams*
(San Francisco: John Wiley & Sons, 2010).

13. Peter Coleman, *The Five Percent: Finding Solutions to Seemingly Impossible
Conflicts* (New York: PublicAffairs, 2011).

14. Linda L. Putnam, "Transformations and Critical Moments in Negotiations," *Negotiation Journal* 20, no. 2 (2004): 275–295; Aaron T. Wolf,
*The Spirit of Dialogue: Lessons from Faith Traditions in Transforming Con-
flict* (Washington, DC: Island Press, 2017).

15. E. Franklin Dukes, Marina A. Piscolish, and John B. Stephens, *Reaching for Higher Ground in Conflict Resolution* (San Francisco: Jossey Bass,
2000); Chris Ernst and Donna Chrobot-Mason, *Boundary Spanning*

Leadership: Six Practices for Solving Problems, Driving Innovation, and Transforming Organizations (New York: McGraw Hill Professional, 2010).

16. Roger Fisher and Daniel Shapiro, *Beyond Reason: Using Emotions as You Negotiate* (New York: Penguin, 2005), 32.

17. Roger Fisher, William L. Ury, and Bruce Patton, *Getting to Yes: Negotiating Agreement without Giving In* (New York: Penguin, 2011).

18. Marc J. Stern and Timothy D. Baird, "Trust Ecology and the Resilience of Natural Resource Management Institutions," *Ecology and Society* 20, no. 2 (2015): 14, http://dx.doi.org/10.5751/ES-07248-200214; Marc J. Stern and Kimberly J. Coleman, "The Multidimensionality of Trust: Applications in Collaborative Natural Resource Management," *Society & Natural Resources* 28, no. 2 (2015): 117–132; Nicole Gillespie and Graham Dietz, "Trust Repair after an Organization-Level Failure," *Academy of Management Review* 34, no. 1 (2009): 127–145, http://dx.doi.org/10.5465/AMR .2009.35713319.

19. Ronald A. Heifetz, *Leadership without Easy Answers* (Cambridge: Harvard University Press, 1998), 22.

20. Ros Tennyson, "The Partnering Toolbook," The Partnering Initiative, 2011, https://thepartneringinitiative.org/publications/toolbook-series/the -partnering-toolbook/; "Engagement Checklist," WWF and Coca Cola, http://wwfcocacolapartnership.com/wp-content/uploads/documents /checklist.pdf.

Chapter 7: Adapting to Change, Uncertainty, and Failure

1. Jamie Holmes, *Nonsense: The Power of Not Knowing* (New York: Crown, 2015); David Epstein, *Range: Why Generalists Triumph in a Specialized World* (New York: Riverhead Books, 2019).

2. A rich body of literature advances and applies similar sensemaking frameworks, for example, The Natural Step, 5-Level Framework, http://www .thenaturalstep.org/5-levels/; Eliot Metzger et al., sSWOT: A Sustainability SWOT, World Resources Institute, https://www.wri.org/publication /sswot; Alan AtKisson, *The ISIS Agreement: How Sustainability Can Improve Organizational Performance and Transform the World* (London, Earthscan, 2012); Peter Senge, Bryan Smith, Nina Kruschwitz, Joe Laur, and Sara Schley, *The Necessary Revolution: Working Together to Create a Sustainable World* (New York, Crown Business, 2010).

3. BSR, "Five-Step Approach to Stakeholder Engagement," 2019, https://

www.bsr.org/en/our-insights/report-view/stakeholder-engagement-five
-step-approach-toolkit; Kammi Schmeer, "Stakeholder Analysis Guidelines," PHR, Abt Associates, 1999, https://www.who.int/workforcealliance
/knowledge/toolkit/33.pdf.

4. Kevin Moss, "The Four Dimensions of Sustainability," Fast Company,
2009, http://admin.csrwire.com/system/report_pdfs/752/original/1236
030087_Four_Dimensions_of_Sustainability_White_Paper.pdf.

5. Donella Meadows, "Leverage points," Academy for System Change,
1999, http://donellameadows.org/archives/leverage-points-places-to
-intervene-in-a-system/.

6. Sheila Jasanoff et al., "Conversations with the Community: AAAS at the
Millennium," *Science* 278, no. 5346 (1997): 2066–2067.

7. Bryan G. Norton, *Sustainable Values, Sustainable Change: A Guide to
Environmental Decision Making* (Chicago: University of Chicago Press,
2015).

8. Jamie E. McFadden, Tim L. Hiller, and Andrew J. Tyre, "Evaluating
the Efficacy of Adaptive Management Approaches: Is There a Formula
for Success?" *Journal of Environmental Management* 92, no. 5 (2011):
1354–1359.

9. Resources and consultancies supporting innovation can be found at
IDEO.com; CoCreative, wearecocreative.com/; Ashoka, ashoka.org/; and
Stanford Social Innovation Review, ssir.org/.

10. Brian Walker and David Salt, *Resilience Thinking: Sustaining Ecosystems
and People in a Changing World* (Washington, DC: Island Press, 2012).

11. Samuel P. Hays, *Conservation and the Gospel of Efficiency* (Pittsburgh:
University of Pittsburgh Press, 1959); Samuel P. Hays, *Beauty, Health, and
Permanence: Environmental Politics in the United States 1955–1985* (New
York: Cambridge University Press, 1987).

12. American Planning Association, "Scenario Planning," accessed June 27,
2020, https://www.planning.org/knowledgebase/scenarioplanning/; Garry
D. Peterson, Graeme S. Cumming, and Stephen R. Carpenter, "Scenario
Planning: A Tool for Conservation in an Uncertain World," *Conservation
Biology* 17, no. 2 (2003): 358–366; Gill Ringland, *Scenario Planning:
Managing for the Future* (New York: John Wiley & Sons, 1998).

13. Ronald A. Heifetz, *Leadership without Easy Answers* (Cambridge, MA:
Harvard University Press, 1994), 99; Stephen Denning, *Squirrel Inc.: A*

Fable of Leadership through Storytelling (San Francisco: Jossey-Bass, 2004); Peter Senge, Hal Hamilton, and John Kania, "Dawn of Systems Leadership," *Stanford Social Innovation Review*, Winter 2015, https://ssir.org /articles/entry/the_dawn_of_system_leadership#.

14. Aaron Antonovsky, *Unraveling the Mystery of Health: How People Manage to Stress and Stay Well* (San Francisco: Jossey Bass, 1987).

Chapter 9: Changing Tastes: Influencing Identity and Choices for Sustainable Food

1. Changing Tastes is a private consultancy that works at the intersection of food services, agriculture, sustainability, public health, and demographics. It advises major corporations, as well as early-stage growth companies, philanthropic institutions, and government agencies in North America and Europe. Menus of Change emerged as a collaboration between Changing Tastes, The Culinary Institute of America, and Harvard's TH Chan School of Public Health. Its mission is to integrate optimal nutrition, environmental stewardship, and social responsibility within the foodservice industry. Its signature event is the only annual industry-wide conference that targets executive actors and helps them integrate nutrition and sustainability and rethink protein as the center of the plate.

2. List: https://www.plantforward50.com/about; cookbook: https://www .plantforward50.com/cookbooks; competition: http://www.menusof change.org/principles-resources/news/more-plant-forward-recipesrevealed -get-inspired-by-the-inaugural-health-car.

3. Menus of Change, tip sheet and Annual Report, 2018, http://www .menusofchange.org/.

Chapter 11: Collective Impact for Climate Mitigation

1. Aspects of this case study appear in R. Bruce Hull and Richard Dooley, "Collective Impact for Climate Mitigation," *Solutions* 10, no. 3 (2019): 29–35.

2. Benjamin R. Barber, *Cool Cities: Urban Sovereignty and the Fix for Global Warming* (New Haven: Yale University Press, 2017); Michael Bloomberg and Carl Pope, *Climate of Hope: How Cities, Businesses, and Citizens Can Save the Planet* (New York: St. Martin's Press, 2017).

3. Arlington County's Community Energy Plan, https://environment.arling tonva.us/energy/. See also Department of Energy Guide to Community

Energy Strategic Planning, https://www.energy.gov/eere/slsc/guide-com
munity-energy-strategic-planning; ICLEI's Emissions Management Program, http://icleiusa.org/programs/emissions-management/.

4. Paul Ferguson and Jay Fisette chaired the board of supervisors and wrote
an informative article about this process: Jay Fisette and Paul Ferguson,
"Arlington County Rethinks Energy," *Live Better Magazine* 33 (January/
February 2014), http://livebettermagazine.com/article/arlington-county
-rethinks-energy/. Ron Carlee, Marsha Allgeier, and Barbara Donnellan
served within county government as county manager, deputy manager,
and assistant county manager, respectively. Kevin Shooshan was an
engaged and influential real estate developer.

Chapter 12: Innovating Carbon Farming

1. https://www.wearecocreative.com/who-we-are.

2. Ken Roseboro, "Indiana Farmer Offers Practical Example of How Soil
Health Can Transform Agriculture," *Green America*, March/April 2019,
https://www.greenamerica.org/story/rick-clark.

Chapter 13: Accounting Makes Sustainability Possible, Profitable, and Boring

1. *Newsweek* ranks Host among the most green businesses: #69 and rising.
Also, Host is listed in DJSI (Dow Jones Sustainability Indices) North
America, is a GRESB (Global Real Estate Sustainability Benchmark) #1
ranked US/Listed company, and shows up consistently in CDP (Carbon
Disclosure Project) rankings of leading businesses.

Chapter 14: Fire Learning Network

1. William Hale Butler and Bruce Evan Goldstein, "The US Fire Learning
Network: Springing a Rigidity Trap through Multiscalar Collaborative
Networks," *Ecology and Society* 15, no. 3 (2010): 21.

2. Bob Lalasz, "The Fire Learning Network Goes under the Microscope,"
Conservation Gateway, March 3, 2011, https://www.conservationgate-
way.org/News/Pages/fire-learning-network-goe.aspx.

Chapter 15: Partnering for Clean Water and Community Benefit

1. This case is adapted from R. Bruce Hull and Seth Brown, "Partnering for
Green Infrastructure," *Solutions* 9 (2019): 3.

2. D. Lueckenhoff and Seth Brown, "Public–Private Partnerships Beneficial for Implementing Green Infrastructure," *Water Law & Policy Monitor,* 2015, https://www.epa.gov/sites/production/files/2016-02/documents /green_inf_bna_cbp3_article.pdf.